I0759661

THE AMAZING GENERATION

Your GUIDE to FUN and FREEDOM in a SCREEN-FILLED WORLD

Written by
JONATHAN HAIDT
and CATHERINE PRICE

Illustrated by CYNTHIA YUAN CHENG

Rocky Pond Books

To our children and their fellow rebels
—J.H. and C.P.

For the bright, creative, inspiring, and amazing kids of the next generation and beyond! —C.Y.C.

ROCKY POND BOOKS
An imprint of Penguin Random House LLC
1745 Broadway, New York, NY 10019
penguinrandomhouse.com

Text written by Jonathan Haidt and Catherine Price
copyright © 2025 by Jonathan Haidt
Graphic novel and other illustrations copyright © 2025 by Cynthia Yuan Cheng
Hand lettering by Mary Kate McDevitt
Art colored by Xanthe Bouma

Penguin Random House values and supports copyright. Copyright fuels creativity, encourages diverse voices, promotes free speech, and creates a vibrant culture. Thank you for buying an authorized edition of this book and for complying with copyright laws by not reproducing, scanning, or distributing any part of it in any form without permission. You are supporting writers and allowing Penguin Random House to continue to publish books for every reader. Please note that no part of this book may be used or reproduced in any manner for the purpose of training artificial intelligence technologies or systems.

Rocky Pond Books and the Rocky Pond Books colophon are registered trademarks of Penguin Random House LLC.

Design by Maya Tatsukawa
Text set in Emy Slab, Something Weird, and SS Pretzel

Library of Congress Cataloging-in-Publication Data is available.

First published in the United States of America by Rocky Pond Books, 2025

Manufactured in the United States of America

ISBN 9798217111909 (hardcover) • 10 9 8 7 6 5 4 3
ISBN 9798217111916 (paperback) • 10 9

The authorized representative in the EU for product safety and compliance is Penguin Random House Ireland, Morrison Chambers, 32 Nassau Street, Dublin D02 YH68, Ireland, https://eu-contact.penguin.ie.

CONTENTS

INTRODUCTION
INTRODUCTION
THE TECH WIZARDS'
AND THEIR LIES
SECRETS OF THE TECH WIZARDS
HOW TO BE A REBEL
CONCLUSION
13

The Greedy Wizards and the Curse of the Stones

Once upon a time, a group of wizards created magical, glowing stones studded with glittering gems. They promised that these stones would bring ***friendship, freedom, and fun*** *to anyone who picked one up. People rushed to grab them, and before long, anyone without a stone felt left out.*

Some of the wizards tried to live up to their promises, but others became greedy. Instead of making life better, they tricked people into carrying their stones with them everywhere they went, and gazing into them all day long. Why? Because these greedy wizards had figured out how to turn human energy into gold.

The more time people spent looking at their stones, the richer the greedy wizards became—and the more ***their promises began to seem like lies.***

Instead of finding friendship, people began to feel lonely. Instead of having fun, they felt anxious and sad. Instead of finding freedom, they felt controlled by their stones.

But then, ***something amazing happened:*** *A few brave young people found the strength to look up. All around* them, they saw people standing motionless, trapped by their stones—and they decided to break free.

These young rebels began hanging out, going on adventures, and doing things they'd loved to do before they fell under the stones' spell. Every experience they had together made them feel more confident and connected. And the more fun they had, the stronger they became.

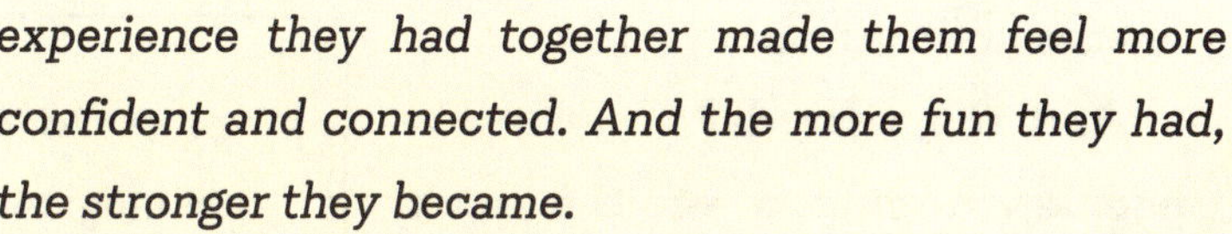

Other kids and teenagers heard the rebels' laughter and decided to join them. The greedy wizards, terrified their power might be slipping away, began to pack even more tricks into the stones. But for the first time ever, the wizards faced resistance.

Today, this rebellion is growing. On one side are the greedy wizards, desperate to keep stealing people's energy so that they can get richer. On the other side are the rebels: young people who have wised up to the wizards' tricks and who want to keep their energy for themselves. The winner of this struggle will determine what life is like not just for their generation, but for generations to come.

So which side will win?

The answer depends on you.

The Real-Life Rebellion

This isn't just a fairy tale. As you've probably figured out, the **glowing stones in the story are smartphones.**

The **glittering gems are apps, websites, and video games** that promise more friendship, freedom, and fun, but are actually designed to steal people's time and energy and turn them into money.

And **the wizards?** They're **the people in charge of the tech companies** that design and sell smartphones, apps, social media platforms, and games.

Not all phones are magical stones—just *smart*phones.

Now, to be clear, *most* people who work at those companies are good people who make useful—often amazing—products. Many got into the business because they wanted to use technology to make life better. And in a lot of ways, technology *does* make life better.

But along the way, some of the leaders of these companies began to care more about making money than anything else. They cared so much about making more money that they were willing to do things that could hurt people (including kids!) as long as *they* kept getting richer. These are the "greedy wizards."

Meet the Rebels

The **rebels are real, too**: They're an **amazing generation** of young people who know how to use technology in ways that help themselves, not greedy tech wizards. They choose to live in the real world as much as possible, and they think for themselves instead of mindlessly following the crowd.

It's easy to spot the rebels: They're not sitting around like zombies, scrolling and swiping. They're out in the world, *doing* things—and as a result, their lives are full of *real* friendships, *real* freedom, and *real* fun.

Interested in joining the rebels? **This book is your guide.**

THE REBELS' CODE

- **Use TECHNOLOGY as a TOOL—DON'T LET technology use YOU**
- **FILL your LIFE with REAL FRIENDSHIP, FREEDOM, and FUN**

All Rebels Are Different

Some rebels love big groups of people, and some like being alone, or with a few close friends. Some are leaders who *start* movements and organizations and convince other people to join them. Others rebel through their *personal* decisions, like choosing to wait to get a smartphone or social media account, or by deciding to spend more time on real-life hobbies and less on screens. No two rebels are the same. And anyone can be a rebel—including you.

You can still become a rebel if you already have a smartphone, tablet, social media account, or video game console. Keep reading to learn how.

I started to cut back on my social media use about six months ago. I'm reading and sleeping more. I'm thinking more independently. I have more time for me. *—Bristal, 15*

I don't feel the need for a phone. I like being with people in the real world, face-to-face. *—Shiloh, 12*

The generation just above yours (born between about 1996 and 2012) = GEN Z

Your generation (born between about 2013 and 2025) = GEN ALPHA

There are also many people from the generation *above* yours who got smartphones and social media when they were around your age (or spent a ton of time gaming), ended up regretting it, and decided to become rebels as young adults. These older rebels want to tell you what they wish they'd known at your age, so that **you can avoid their mistakes** . . .

I missed out on my entire teenagehood because of social media and my phone. *—Kayleigh, 25*

I really wish I had gotten to know my grandfather better before he died, instead of always playing video games when he visited. *—Benjamin, 21*

. . . and how **joining the rebellion has made their lives better.**

> I'm having more fun and doing more exciting things. I'm also better able to remember how I actually spent my time.
>
> *—Alyssa, 26*

All of the rebels want to share advice with you and your friends about how **you can become rebels too.**

> I've rediscovered hobbies that truly fulfill me.
>
> *—Sophia, 21*

MEET a REBEL

SAMARA GORTON

18 years old, New York

First smartphone? When I was 11.

Ah-ha moment?

I went to a sleepaway camp that was phone free, and I loved it.

Inspiration / role models?

One of my friends *chose* to have a time limit on her phone. If she wanted more time, she had to call her dad to get the password. I thought that was smart–so I did it too.

Advice for your younger self?

I would never get TikTok. I hate Instagram and Snapchat. I wish they didn't exist. They're not cool.

What do you wish kids knew?

It might look like teens are entranced by their phones and social media, but a lot of them are not enjoying it and they wish they weren't on it.

What do you do with your free time?

I love tennis. I love to run. I'm learning to play guitar. And I like film photography a lot. It encourages me to look for the beauty around me.

Advice for young rebels?

A lot of growing up is about self-discovery, and I just don't think you'll ever find yourself through your phone.

JAX

Likes skating, building

SOPHIE

Likes playing guitar, science

This book is two books in one: the main book, and a graphic novel, which is fictional but is based on real kids. Here's how it starts.

ALEX

Likes funny videos, skating

EMMA

Likes photography, crafts

DAVID

Likes gaming, playing piano

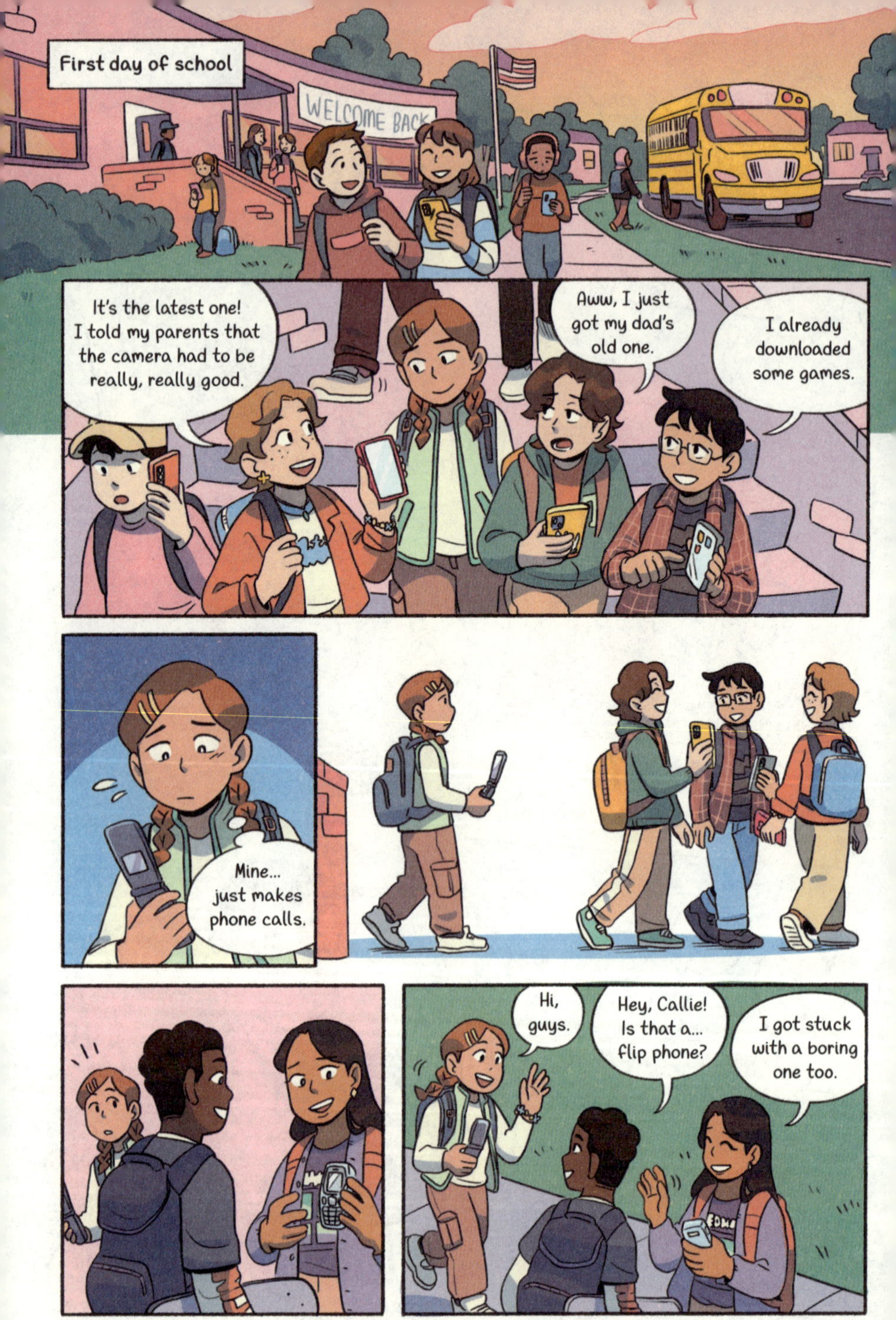

First day of school

WELCOME BACK

It's the latest one! I told my parents that the camera had to be really, really good.

Aww, I just got my dad's old one.

I already downloaded some games.

My mom says I can't have a smartphone until at least high school.
Yeah, I tried to convince my parents too, but no luck.
Hey, at least you have one!
I still have to ask the guys at the skate park to borrow their phones. It's so embarrassing...
SIGH...
Later...
ding!
Hey, Emma!
Want to hang out at the park?
Callie!
Um...
Sorry, today's busy. Maybe another time?
Oh! Yeah, okay...
...Bye.

Over the weekend...

First live!
Hi everyone!

LIVE 15

alextheskater hiiii emma
alextheskater spamming ur chat now
alextheskater spamspamspamspam
not_david hahahaha
matt.r2k my fave is the puppy filter :) give it a try!

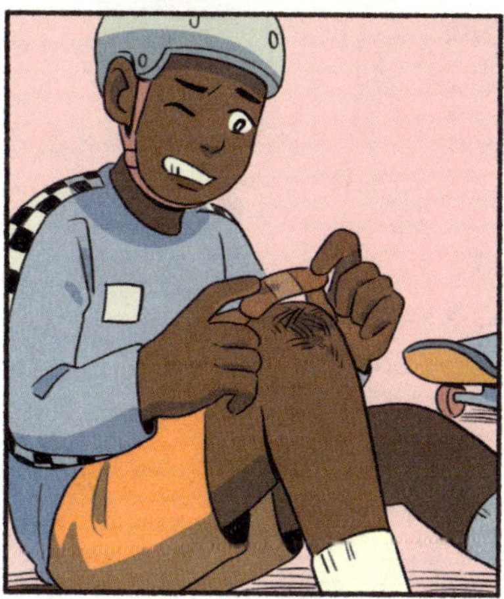

alextheskater grabbing bagels with @em4ever !
not_david
not_david 5 wins in a row. getting pretty good at this
VICTORY
1
2
3
alextheskater
em4ever nice work!

ha
I withdrew from my family and real-life friends, choosing to prioritize online friends over everything else. But the more I felt connected to someone across the country, the less I felt connected to the people right next to me. —Mia, 19

PART ONE

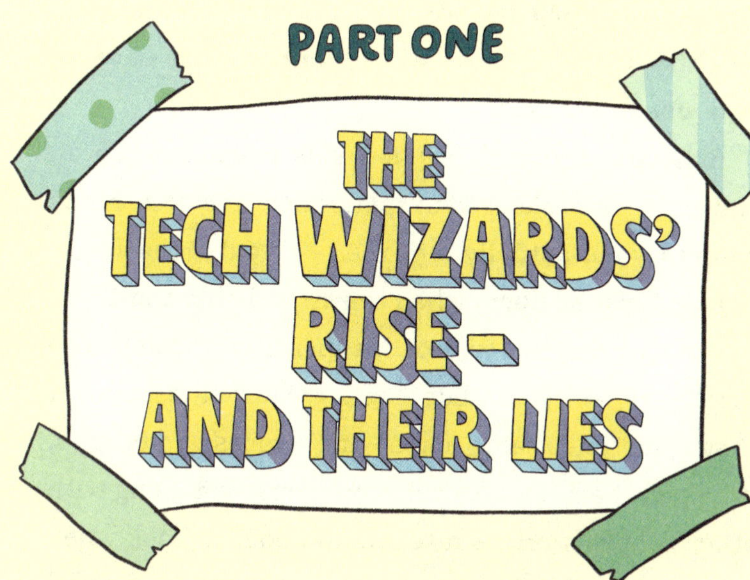

THE TECH WIZARDS' RISE—AND THEIR LIES
SECRETS OF THE TECH WIZARDS
HOW TO BE A REBEL
CONCLUSION

Can you imagine leaving your house on your own, meeting up with friends, and roaming around your neighborhood for hours while your parents have no idea where you are?

Believe it or not, this is how kids as young as seven and eight years old used to spend their free time. Many parents would actually send their kids out of the house, saying, "Just be home when the streetlights come on."

Not only was this type of unsupervised and unstructured play really fun, but it was great for kids, even if they sometimes came home with scrapes and bruises. It helped them learn to solve problems, get along with other people, work as a team, and bounce back when things didn't go their way. It also helped them build confidence and independence, because they got to test their limits and learn from their mistakes and failures.

On weekends and evenings, my brother and I would spend hours playing games in our rural Maryland backyard with our friends: hide-and-seek games with complicated rules, water balloon fights, and endless races. In the fall, we'd jump in leaf piles, and in the winter, we'd have snowball fights and make snowmen. When it was raining, we'd take our games inside. We had no phones and only three TV channels. —*Sophia, born 1986*

When we were nine, my best friend and I built a shack in my backyard out of bits of lumber we took from a construction site, so that we could hide away from my parents and keep a stash of candy. It felt so great to have a clubhouse, which we built with our own hands. *—Jon, born 1963*

I grew up in New York City, and my friends and I would play on the swings or the monkey bars or play games in the street. Even when I was seven or eight years old, I used to bike to Central Park on my own and ride around the park or rent ice skates. Kids would go home when it got dark. I loved having freedom. *—Mary, born 1942*

TRY THIS!

Ask your own parents or grandparents what they used to do in the afternoon when they came home from school, or on weekends, or summer vacation. What was the most fun?

DID YOU KNOW?

Humans and other mammals aren't the only creatures that play. Scientists have seen playful behavior in everything from birds to fish to reptiles. For example, **baby alligators have been seen sliding down muddy banks as if they're waterslides!** * If so many different types of animals spend time playing when they are young, it must be important.

* You can find the source or link for every claim about research or science at AmazingGeneration.com.

Playing Puts You into "Discover" Mode

Another reason that playing without anyone watching you or telling you what to do is important is that it puts you into **"discover mode":** a confident, curious, fun state of mind where **you feel free** to take risks and push your limits. Every time you try something new or challenging and succeed (or even fail, but bounce back), you'll feel a little braver trying new things in the future. And if you spend a lot of time in discover mode when you're a kid and teenager, you'll be more likely to stay in it as a grown-up.

September
Hillside Skate Park
Hey, Alex! I didn't know you skate too!
Er, yeah... I just got a board.
Let me know if you want to practice together! I'll be by the ramp.
Th-thanks...
HUP!
SL IP!
OOF!

Sigh...

how to get good at skateboarding fast
Search
tap
tap

5 TIPS for beginner skaters

COOLEST STREET SKATING

World Champ Skate Highligh...

Whoa...
Yo, Jax!
Check out
this video...
YES!
That trick
was so cool!!
Do it again,
I wanna take
a video!

So why do many kids in *your* generation spend so little time playing outside with friends, and so much *more* time inside and alone—often on screens? In other words, why did **"play-based childhoods"** get replaced by **"phone-based childhoods"?**

There are many reasons, but here are two of the biggest:

Beginning in the 1980s, many parents started getting nervous about letting their kids play out of the house unsupervised. Partly because of shows they saw on TV, parents worried that strangers would hurt their kids, even though crime rates in the U.S. began falling sharply in the 1990s. So they kept their kids inside.

In the meantime, **screens got more appealing, more numerous . . . and more addictive.**

> **The Great Rewiring of Childhood** is the name for this giant shift in how kids and teenagers spent their time.

What Was Technology Like When Your Parents and Grandparents Were Kids?

It wasn't like there were no screens when your parents and grandparents were kids. But things were *very* different.

People watched **TV,** but you couldn't stream shows anytime you wanted (there was no Netflix or YouTube). Instead, you had to watch whatever was on at that moment.

If you wanted to see a **movie,** you had to go to a theater or rent one from a video store. If someone else had already rented the movie you wanted, too bad: You had to pick something else—or wait for them to return it.

Video games existed, but there was usually no way to chat with other players while you were playing the game unless they were in the room with you.

And **phones?** Before the late 1990s, most people only had **landlines**—phones that had to be plugged into the wall. If you left the house, no one could call you. If kids needed to contact

their parents, they had to use a friend's or neighbor's landline, or find a **phone booth**—a little glass closet with a pay phone inside. (You had to remember to bring coins to pay for the call!)

During the school day, the only way for parents to reach their kids was to leave a message with the school office, and the only way for kids to contact their parents was to go to the school office and ask to use the phone.

Almost no one had access to the **internet** until the 1990s. In those early days, if you wanted to go online, you had to connect your computer to your phone line or go to an internet café to rent time on a computer. **Wi-Fi** (wireless internet) didn't spread widely until the early 2000s—and it was way too slow to stream videos.

The first **cell (or mobile) phones** started becoming popular in the early 2000s, and

TRY THIS!

Ask your parents if they ever had a computer that connected to the internet using a modem and a phone line. If so, ask them to imitate the sound the modem made as it connected.

(Brace yourself: They may make an extremely odd noise.)

most people used them just to make calls and send short **text messages.** Why short? Because they didn't have touch screens; instead, you had to spell words out letter by letter using the numeric keypad. (For example, to type the letter *C* you had to press the 2 key three times. It was practically Morse code.)

The **first social media platforms** popped up in the early 2000s and became popular quickly, but they were websites, not apps, so the only way to spend time on them was to sit in front of a computer. (They also only showed you updates from people you had chosen to follow.) And since many people still used film cameras (or digital cameras that had to be connected to a computer with a cord) there was no way to snap a selfie and immediately post it for friends and strangers to see.

TRY THIS!

Ask your parents about their first experiences with social media. What was different, compared to today?

WHAT IS SOCIAL MEDIA?

"Social media" is any app or website where people can create profiles and share content (like photos, videos, links, and text) with a big audience, including strangers. Social media platforms let people connect and interact with each other by following accounts, joining groups, commenting, liking, sharing, and sending direct messages. By this definition, Instagram, TikTok, Snapchat, Twitch, Reddit, Discord, and Facebook are all social media. YouTube technically is too, though most people use it just to watch videos.

The Original Glowing Stones

On January 9, 2007, Steve Jobs, the founder and head of Apple, stood onstage at a giant tech convention called MacWorld and made a dramatic announcement:

> ***"Every once in a while, a revolutionary product comes along that changes everything."***
> —Steve Jobs, CEO of Apple

He was unveiling the world's first smartphone: the iPhone. And, as it turned out, he was right: Smartphones *did* change everything, especially for kids.

Three things make smartphones different from earlier technologies, and more powerful.

First, **smartphones are *small*,** which makes it possible for people to pull them out anytime they have even a few seconds of downtime, or feel awkward or bored. Sure, your parents watched TV when they were kids, but they never unplugged their family's television set and carried it around with them, or took it to school.

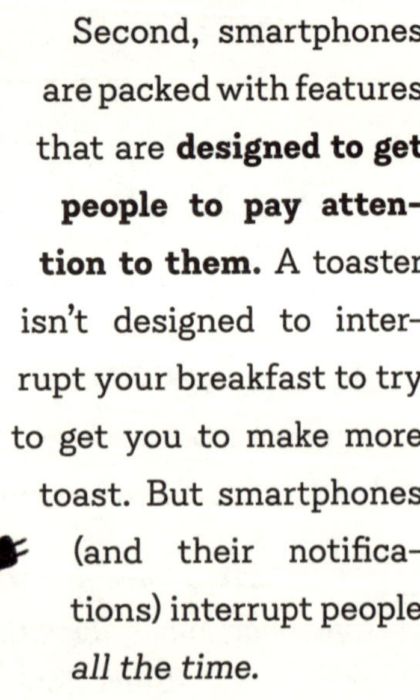

Second, smartphones are packed with features that are **designed to get people to pay attention to them.** A toaster isn't designed to interrupt your breakfast to try to get you to make more toast. But smartphones (and their notifications) interrupt people *all the time.*

Third, smartphones **contain *apps.*** ("App" is short for "application," which is another word for a computer program.) Apps transformed smartphones from basic, practical tools that could only do a limited number of things into the magical stones from our fairy tale, embedded with hundreds of glittering gems.

In 2007, when Steve Jobs announced the first iPhone, he only showed off three of its features to his audience: the telephone, the music player, and the internet browser. But after the first app store was launched in 2008, it became possible for people to download hundreds of apps onto their smartphones. And this meant that smartphones could suddenly do hundreds of different things.

Good Apps and Bad Apps

Many apps are extremely useful and make life easier or better—like apps for making calls, sending texts, keeping track of your calendar, listening to music, or paying for things. These are **"tool" apps,** and they don't tend to cause problems. (Very few people spend hours at a time using their calculator.) If smartphones *only* had tool apps, then they probably would only have changed the world for the better.

But not all apps are designed to be helpful tools. Some apps are deliberately designed to suck up massive amounts of people's time. You can think of these apps as **"time wasters."**

Why would the tech companies make apps like that? Because just like the wizards from the fairy tale, they had figured out how to turn people's time into money—and some of them got greedy. They saw how much money they were making and wanted to make even more. So they figured out ways to make their apps even **harder** to stop using. These time-wasting apps are sometimes called **"addictive-by-design,"** because that's exactly what they are designed to do: hook people.

> ***"The thought process that went into building these [social media] applications . . . was all about: 'How do we consume as much of your time and conscious attention as possible?'"***
>
> —Sean Parker, first president of Facebook

A lot of apps can waste your time or hook you, but there are four types of apps that are *especially* powerful and that rebels know to watch out for: **social media apps** like Instagram, Snapchat, and TikTok, **video platforms** like YouTube, **games** and **gaming platforms** like Roblox, and **AI chatbot apps** like Character.AI and Replika.

DID YOU KNOW?

Some apps are especially tricky because they can be useful tools *and* addictive time wasters. For example, YouTube can be a great learning tool, but it's also designed to make it hard to stop watching videos once you start.

The Tech Wizards' Spell Became More Sinister

"When Facebook was getting going, I had these people who came up to me and they would say, 'I'm not on social media. . . . I value my real-life interactions, I value the moment, I value presence, I value intimacy.' And I would say 'We'll get you eventually.'"
—Sean Parker, first president of Facebook

Soon, young people were rushing to get smartphones and download apps, especially social media apps, and were spending hours every day using them. This left them with a lot *less* time for the things kids used to do (and that scientists know are really important) like **playing together in person, spending time outside, exercising, and sleeping.**

Now, to be clear, a lot of the people in the generation above yours are happy and thriving.

But many of them are struggling. By 2015, a startling number of young people around the world were feeling worried and sad a lot (or even most) of the time. Many of them felt so bad that they needed professional help from therapists and psychiatrists. Some young people began to wonder if there might be a connection between their struggles and the amount of time they were spending on smartphones and social media. Scientists did too.

DID YOU KNOW?

By 2024, the U.S. Surgeon General had become so convinced that using social media was bad for teenagers' mental health that he said social media apps should come with warning labels, like the ones on cigarettes.

SOCIAL MEDIA, SMARTPHONES, AND MENTAL HEALTH: WHAT DOES THE SCIENCE SAY?

When people spend a lot of time on social media and other apps that have been designed to be addictive, it makes them more likely to be depressed and anxious.

For example, scientific studies have found that:

- Girls who spend five or more hours each day on social media (which is surprisingly common!) are *three times* more likely to be depressed than girls who spend little or no time on social media.
- Boys who spend five or more hours a day on social media are *two times* more likely to be depressed than boys who spend little or no time on social media.
- When young adults who usually spend a lot of time on social media spend less time on it for a few weeks, they usually feel happier and less anxious.
- When people block the internet on their smartphones, so that they can just use them as *phones*, most of them feel better and say that it's easier for them to concentrate and pay attention to things.

The Tech Wizards' False Promises

FRIENDSHIP

The tech wizards had promised that their products would bring people more friendship, and young people did use smartphones and social media to stay in touch and meet new people with similar interests or backgrounds. But strangely, as soon as most young people got smartphones and began spending a lot more time on social media (in the early 2010s), rates of loneliness began to *rise*, not fall, as you can see in this graph:

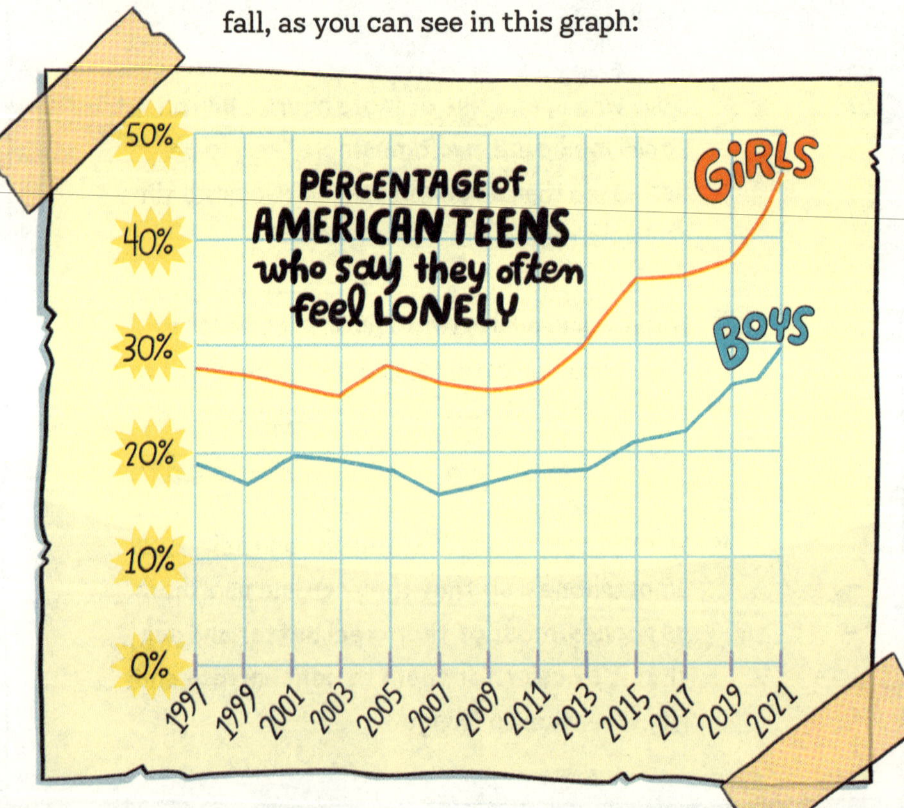

It makes sense that kids and teenagers who didn't have smartphones or social media started to feel lonely: Their friends weren't available to play or hang out because they were too busy staring at their phones.

But it wasn't just the kids who *didn't* have smartphones who felt lonely. **The kids who *did* have smartphones started saying that they felt lonely too**—which was the exact opposite of what the tech companies had promised their products would do!

Social media made me very isolated.
—Ruqayah, 16

Making things worse, some kids started using social media and group text chains to hurt each other by spreading rumors, bullying classmates, and saying nasty things—not a great recipe for friendship.

I started to have private photos sent around of me without my consent in Snapchat group chats by a famous influencer on TikTok and got harassed on the day-to-day, with everyone picking apart my face and body.
—Calla, 22

FREEDOM

The wizards had promised that their products would give people freedom. But oddly, the more time kids and teenagers spent on them, the less free—and more trapped and anxious—many of them felt.

I was a huge gamer in elementary school. It was an exciting escape. But my habit of escaping kept me from spending time on other things, like learning the guitar or getting over my "beginner's anxiety" when I tried to play sports. *—Nick, 24*

I felt like I couldn't exist without my smartphone.
—Kate, 24

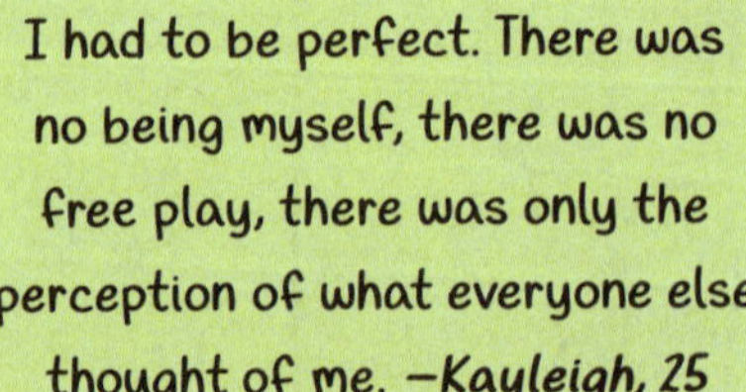

I had to be perfect. There was no being myself, there was no free play, there was only the perception of what everyone else thought of me. *—Kayleigh, 25*

What's more, many parents had assumed that allowing their kids to spend their free time inside alone on smartphones was safer than letting them play outside with friends, but it turned out that this wasn't true either: The tech wizards hadn't done much to make their apps safe for children, and creepy adults started using messaging features in social media apps and video games to contact kids. Many kids and teens felt scared, anxious, and miserable, and their parents often had no idea what was going on online.

> **Many kids were *overprotected* in real life and *under-protected* online.**

DISCOVER MODE VERSUS DEFEND MODE

Feeling trapped and nervous is a sign that your brain is in **"defend mode"**: an anxious and fearful state of mind where your brain is on high alert for anything that might be dangerous.

Defend mode is the opposite of **discover mode**—that confident, curious state of mind mentioned earlier where new things feel exciting, not scary.

Defend mode is essential when you're in situations that are truly dangerous, because it helps keep you safe. But sometimes your brain can flip into defend mode in response to things that feel bad but that aren't *actually* dangerous (like mean comments on social media)—and get stuck in it.

This is probably one reason why so many young people started feeling more anxious and trapped when they stopped playing with friends in person and started spending so much time on smartphones and social media: As they constantly compared themselves to others and worried about what everyone was saying about them, **their brains got pushed from discover mode into defend mode.**

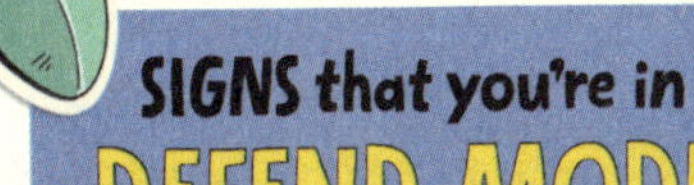

SIGNS that you're in DEFEND MODE	SIGNS that you're in DISCOVER MODE
LIFE seems FULL of THREATS and PROBLEMS	LIFE seems FULL of GOOD THINGS and OPPORTUNITIES
FEELING ANXIOUS or INSECURE	FEELING CURIOUS and HOPEFUL
Wanting to RUN AWAY	Wanting to CHECK THINGS OUT
FEELING OVERWHELMED	FEELING IN CONTROL
BAD thoughts KEEP REPEATING in your MIND	BAD thoughts MAY GO THROUGH your MIND but they don't KEEP REPEATING
Assuming the WORST ABOUT PEOPLE	Giving people the BENEFIT of the DOUBT
THINKING or WORRYING ABOUT the PAST or FUTURE	FEELING PRESENT in the MOMENT
FEELING TRAPPED	FEELING FREE

FUN

The tech wizards had promised that their products would make life more fun, but some early rebels noticed that the *more* time they spent on smartphones and social media, the *less* fun life felt.

> I fell into the trap of content creation. It seemed everything my friends and I did had to be for a "bit." When we hung out, we would try to record everything instead of just having fun. *—Matthew, 19*

> I loved to ride bikes, make up imaginary plays with my siblings, hang out with my friends, and play outside. But after we all got smartphones, everything got transferred to "hanging out" online. It completely changed how we all spent our time. *—Jade, 26*

THE TECH WIZARDS' TRAP

Here's something that may shock you: **Nearly half of people between eighteen and twenty-seven say they wish that some of the most popular social media platforms and apps, such as TikTok, X, and Snapchat, *had never been invented*!**

And yet . . . most young people keep using them. Today, **the average American teenager spends about five hours per day on social media** (including YouTube), and nearly half of teens say that they're online "almost constantly."

DID YOU KNOW?

Ninety-five percent of young adults who have smartphones keep their phone near them almost all the time. (Like in their beds, in the bathroom, and everywhere they go.)

On the surface, this doesn't make any sense: If you dislike something so much that *you wish it had never been invented*, then why would you use it at all, let alone for hours every single day?

For example, if you didn't like bicycles, you definitely wouldn't spend hours a day riding one. And you probably wouldn't wish they'd never even been invented. Instead, you just . . . wouldn't get a bike.

So what's so different about smartphones and social media? Why are so many people in the generation above yours spending so much time using things that they *know* are hurting them, and that many of them would be happy to see disappear?

It's because **they've been tricked and they've been trapped.**

And if *your* generation is going to avoid their fate, **you need to know the truth.**

I'm fifteen with no hobbies, interests, goals, or ambitions. All I do is waste time on my phone. . . . I wanna skateboard, I wanna play an instrument, I want to learn chess . . . I want to do all sorts of things, but I never do. My screen time is near eleven hours daily, and I feel like just . . . crying myself to sleep. How do I stop this crippling addiction I have with my phone? *—Anonymous Reddit user, 15*

I missed out on a lot of social experiences. I didn't go to sporting events. I never had those early youth experiences of "young love." I find myself having difficulty with eye contact and making small talk. I wish I had simply lived life more, rather than allowing myself to be consumed by the addictive online world.

—Matthew, 19

WHY YOU NEED TO KNOW THE TRUTH *RIGHT NOW!*

There are two periods of life when human brains change the most. One was when you were a baby and toddler, when your brain was growing really fast. The other is when you're in adolescence, the period of life between age ten and your early twenties. And your brain changes *especially* fast during puberty, which can begin even before age ten, and which is generally finished by around age sixteen. That means that you're probably in it right now!

The fact that your brain will be so flexible and changeable for the next few years is a superpower, because it means you can learn new things quickly and can absorb huge amounts of information much faster than adults can.

But your brain's flexibility also puts you at risk of being taken advantage of by people or companies who would like to change your brain in ways that help *them*, not you.

That means that out of your entire life, this is the most important time to learn about the tech wizards' secrets and their tricks—and guard your brain against them.

My iPhone preyed on my developing brain. It addicted me and overall made me lonelier and less happy. If I could do it again, I would have waited longer to get a phone. —*Sam, 17*

MEET a REBEL

BEN SPALOSS

22 years old, Nevada

When did you get your first smartphone?

Eighth grade.

Was that too early or too late?

Too early. I thought I needed it to belong, but I didn't.

What did you do on social media?

I posted on TikTok for two years almost every day to help people get off their phones.

How big did it get?

About 250,000 followers. Averaged a couple million views per month.

Why did you stop?

I got my dream job. But I also just wanted a break. It was exhausting, and I wanted more time for myself.

What do you wish more people understood?

Tech companies sell a promise: connection, fun, freedom. But it is a promise they can't keep. What matters is caring for people. Having deep connections.

What makes someone a rebel?

Being willing to be different in order to live better. Seeing the suffering around you and saying, "This isn't how I want to live."

Boo
Alex, can you look a little more excited?

Oh, I missed the photo! Can you redo that?
TRICK OR TREAT
clik

Candy haul! I got one chocolate bar, five Kit Kats...
CHOCO

TRICK OR TREAT!
OoOOH
UWOo
Love your costume!
Aw, more caramel. Jax, want to trade?

Check it out—mine ate too much candy!
That's exactly how I feel right now!
Mine's finished too!
AAAHH!
What do you think? Scary enough?
ha ha!
How did you make that??

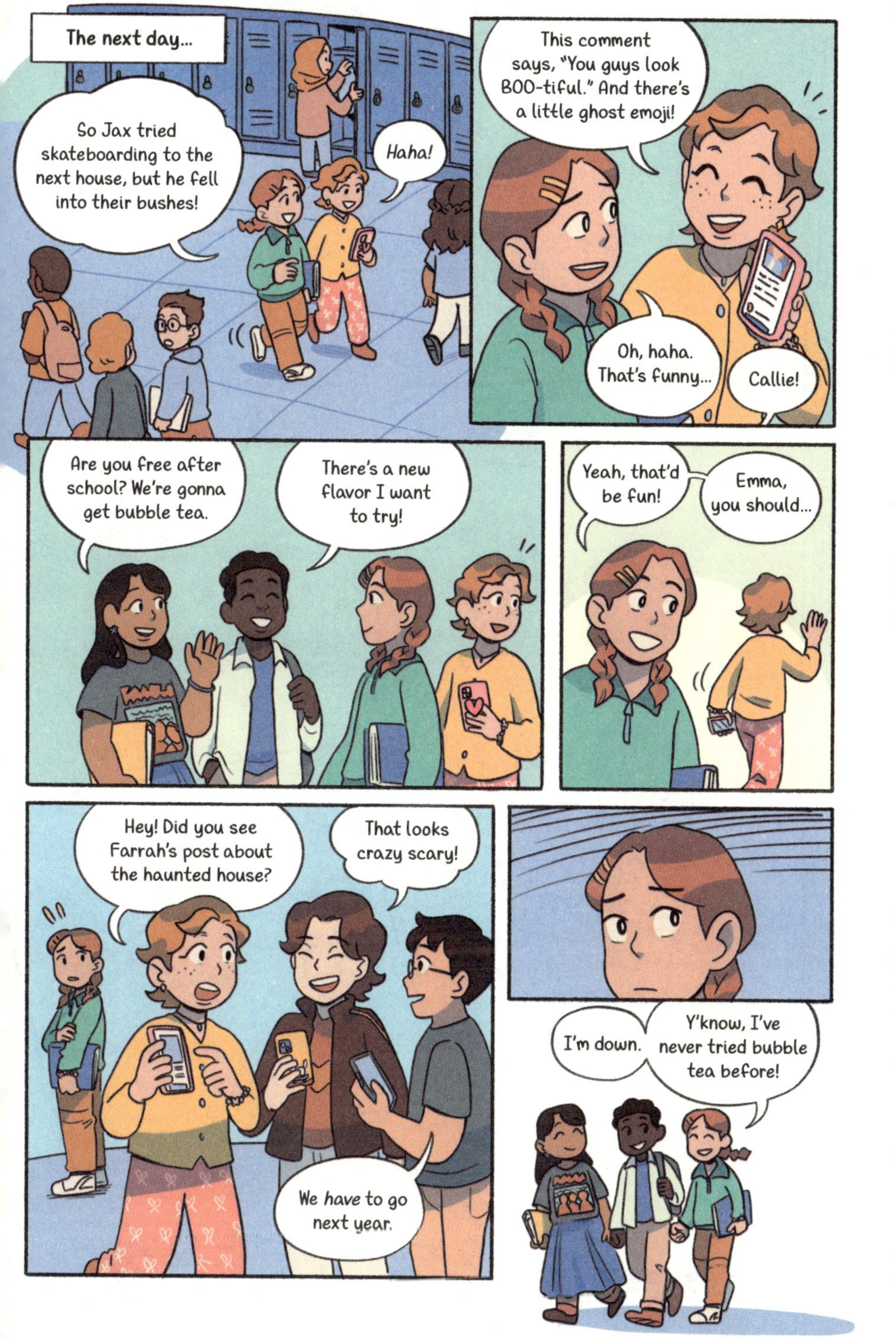

The next day...

So Jax tried skateboarding to the next house, but he fell into their bushes!

Haha!

This comment says, "You guys look BOO-tiful." And there's a little ghost emoji!

Oh, haha. That's funny...

Callie!

Are you free after school? We're gonna get bubble tea.

There's a new flavor I want to try!

Yeah, that'd be fun!

Emma, you should...

Hey! Did you see Farrah's post about the haunted house?

That looks crazy scary!

We *have* to go next year.

BUY
$
SECRET
TECH WIZARD
CONFIDENTIAL
9am-
11am
Watch
videos
12pm-
5:30pm
Scroll on
social me
7pm-
9pm
Play vi
ga
SECRET

SECRETS OF THE TECH WIZARDS

I used to think these companies really wanted the best for me in my life. Now I think they're just using me to make money.

—Gabriela, 23

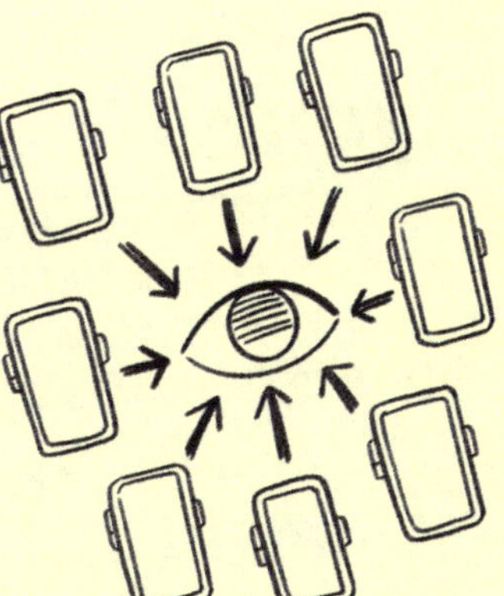

They AREN'T SELLING APPS—
They're SELLING YOU

"FREE" APPS can
COST A LOT

They're HACKING your BRAIN

They're REWIRING your BRAIN

They KNOW their PRODUCTS
ARE HURTING KIDS

Wouldn't it be fun to be the child of a tech wizard? They must get all the latest technology even before their friends see it, right?

Wrong. Instead, **many of the people who run these companies don't let their own children use their products!**

For example:

- The CEO (chief executive officer) of TikTok has said that he doesn't let his own kids use TikTok.
- The CEO of Snapchat limited his kid's screen time to ninety minutes *per week*, and according to his wife, he himself "avoids screens at all times."
- One of the founders of a major video game company called Storm8 says he doesn't let his own kids play the games he's created. He says, "Knowing all the techniques with which we tried to bring about addiction, I realized I didn't want my children exposed to that risk."

* Some tech leaders make their children's babysitters and nannies sign a contract swearing that they will not let the children have contact with smartphones, games, or any screens at all.

If this sounds strange to you, it's because it *is* strange. It turns out that the technology executives know a lot of things about their products that they don't want *you* to know—and **it's time for those secrets to be revealed.**

SECRET #1
The TECH WIZARDS aren't SELLING APPS—they're SELLING *YOU*

Smartphone and social media companies are some of the richest companies in the entire history of the world. For example, Meta (which owns Instagram, Facebook, WhatsApp, and Threads) is worth more than a trillion dollars. That's a *million* millions: $1,000,000,000,000.

Now, it makes sense that companies that sell *smartphones* are worth a lot of money, because smartphones are expensive and lots of people buy them. But Meta and other social media companies like Snap and TikTok don't make smartphones—they make apps. And their apps are free to download and use. So **how are these companies worth so much money?**

That's the first secret that the tech wizards don't want you to know: Their companies don't make money by selling apps.

They make their money by showing you ads in your feed. Every time you pay attention to an ad, even for a split second, the company that made the ad pays money to the

> **DID YOU KNOW?**
>
> If you worked at a job that paid you $100,000 a year, earning a trillion dollars would take you *ten million years.*

social media wizards. The more time you spend on the app, the more ads the social media wizards can show you and the more money they make. In other words, social media wizards make money by **selling your time and attention** to companies that want to show you ads.

This means that you're not the customer. **You're the product that's being sold.**

YOUR TIME AND ATTENTION = MONEY FOR THE WIZARDS

When you're not on apps:

Social media company:

When you see an ad on an app:

Social media company:

$

When you press on the ad:

Social media company:

$ $ $

Here's an example of how this system works:

1. A company has something it wants to sell, like skateboards.
2. That company makes ads for its skateboards.
3. The social media company figures out who might be interested in buying a skateboard.
4. The social media company puts skateboard ads into those people's feeds.
5. Every time someone looks at an ad—even for a second—the skateboard company pays the social media company money, because now they have a potential customer. And if the person *clicks* on the ad, the skateboard company pays the social media company more.

The Attention Economy

This system—where companies make money by selling your time and attention to *other* companies—is called **"the attention economy."** Any app that has ads is most likely a part of it.

Not all ads are obvious. Posts and videos that are labeled as "sponsored" are always ads. So are many things that are labeled as "suggested for you." Those

CONSIDER THIS:

Every minute you spend on social media—or any other app with ads—is a minute spent making money for a tech wizard.

things are in people's feeds because a company or person is paying to put them there. Same thing if an influencer on social media starts talking about one of their "favorite" products: They are probably being paid to do that. There's no way to know whether they really like the product they're trying to get you to buy.

In fact, there's often no way to tell whether *anything* you see on social media is true. Why? Because **social media companies don't check to make sure that the things people post on their platforms are accurate—or even real.** Their goal isn't to tell the truth. It's to make money from ads. That's why it's important to get into the habit of asking ***why* you're being shown particular posts and ads, *who's* paying for them, and *what* they're trying to get you to do.**

TRY THIS!

Ask someone who uses Instagram if you can look through the first ten posts in their feed. Count how many of them are labeled as "sponsored" or "suggested for you." (This means they're probably ads.) Tell them and see how they react.

HOW DO VIDEO GAME CREATORS MAKE MONEY?

- **Selling the Game:** Some games are sold for a one-time price: You buy the game (either in a store or by downloading it) and then play it as much as you want.
- **Advertising:** Many "free" games make money the same way as social media companies: They show ads to players.
- **In-Game Purchases:** Many games are free to play, but then they push you to buy extra stuff inside the game, like new clothes and "skins" for your character, special powers, extra lives, or new levels.
- **Subscriptions:** Some games or services let you pay a monthly or yearly fee to play lots of games or get extra benefits.

That's the ultimate goal: to build habit-forming games that have players coming back every day. . . .
—William Siu, cofounder of the mobile gaming developer Storm8

- **Downloadable Content (DLC):** After a game is released, sometimes the makers add new content, like new levels or characters, that players can buy separately.

How Do the Tech Wizards Figure Out What Ads to Show You?

Unlike traditional printed newspapers and magazines, which show the same ads and news stories to everyone who reads the paper, social media apps show you content and ads that have been chosen just for you.

The tech wizards use computer programs called **"algorithms"** to decide exactly what to show each person in any given moment. (An algorithm is basically a set of instructions.) That's why **no two people's social media feeds ever look the same:** The algorithm picks different photos, videos, posts, and ads for each person, based on what it calculates is most likely to keep them on the platform. Remember: The more time you spend scrolling, and the more attention you pay to the ads, the more money the wizards make.

So how do the tech wizards and their algorithms figure out exactly what to show you?

Simple: **They spy on you.** The more they know about you (and your friends), the easier it is for them to figure out which ads you're most likely to click on and which content is most likely to

keep you glued to their apps. The tech wizards like to say that their products give people freedom. But rebels know that **smartphones are tracking devices** that the wizards have convinced people to carry with them everywhere they go.

Every time you look at, watch, or post something (or leave a like or a comment), the tech wizards and their algorithms record what you did and use that information to figure out what you're already interested in and what *might* interest you in the future.

CONSIDER THIS:

Imagine that someone approached you on the street and asked you to tell them your name, birthdate, address, the name and address of your school, the names and real-time locations of all your family members and friends, a history of everywhere you'd ever been (and who you were with), and your favorite clothes, music, shows, movies, and foods. Would you tell them?

They also collect information that you probably don't even realize you're sharing. For example, they can record how long you look at a post or video, even tracking tiny pauses that are shorter than the blink of an eye. They can also use the location sensors on your phone to tell where you are and which friends you're hanging out with at any moment. Sometimes they can even figure out your mood.

The social media wizards may *say* that their apps are designed to help "empower people to express themselves, live in the moment, learn about the world, and have fun together" (Snapchat) or "bring you closer to the people and things you love" (Instagram) or "inspire creativity and bring joy" (TikTok).

But rebels know that any company that spies on its users and designs its products to be addictive cannot be trusted. Instead, **the tech wizards' *real* goal is to become richer, and they are willing to harm people (including kids and teenagers) to do it.**

I wish people viewed tech companies with more suspicion and even disgust. —*Jakey, 16*

CONSIDER THIS:

Sarah Wynn-Williams, a former executive at Meta, told the U.S. Congress that **Instagram can detect when teenage girls feel bad about themselves** by, for example, identifying when they delete a few selfies. According to Wynn-Williams, the app then uses that as an opportunity to show the girls ads for beauty products.

YOUR RIGHT TO PRIVACY

Sometimes, when people learn that the wizards are spying on them, they say things like, *"Why would I care about privacy? I've got nothing to hide!"* But in reality, privacy matters. A lot.

- Privacy helps you stay in control of your own life. It means *you* get to decide what people know about you, when they know it, and who gets to know it.

- Privacy lets you be yourself without pressure. When you're not being watched or judged, it's easier to let down your guard, be honest about how you feel, and try new things without worrying about being made fun of if you mess up.

- Privacy keeps you safe. When strangers (or even people you know) have too much personal information about you (or pictures or videos of you), it makes it easier for them to trick you, bother you, or use it against you.

I just don't feel comfortable with having traces of myself on the internet forever.
—Philippa, 23

SECRET #2 "FREE" APPS CAN COST a LOT

Some people say that they don't mind if the tech wizards spy on them, because the apps don't cost money—so they think it's a fair trade. Also, sometimes the apps show them ads and content they're actually interested in.

But rebels know the truth. **These apps *do* cost something: your time and attention.** And that's a big deal because your time and attention are even *more* valuable than money. In fact, they're two of **the most valuable things you have.**

How could time and attention be more valuable than money?

Because if you spend money on something and regret it, you can usually return it or get your money back. But once you spend a

CONSIDER THIS:

You can tell that time and attention are valuable resources because of the words we use to talk about them. When we say that we "spend" time or "pay" attention, we're using the same verbs that we use to talk about money!

moment of your time or attention on something—or let an app take it from you—it's gone forever. You can't use it for anything else, and you can't get it back.

That matters, because **your life is really just a collection of moments**—you can think of it as a jar that you fill up one moment at a time. That means that if you want a life that's fun and meaningful, you have to be picky about what kind of moments you're putting into your jar. In other words, you need to be careful about how you're "spending" your attention and time.

I felt like I was wasting my life. If I live ninety years, but thirty of those years are on my phone, did I really live those ninety years?
—Kailani, 15

Moments are tiny, but they add up to hours, days, weeks, years, and, eventually, your whole life. So exactly how much of their lives are people handing over to the tech wizards?

As you know, American teens spend an average of about **five hours a day on social media** (including watching videos on TikTok and YouTube). **That adds up to two and a half full months every year—the equivalent of their *entire* summer break.**

Add in the additional time they're spending on *other* screens—for example, watching television and visiting websites—and the average rises to more than eight hours on screens every day. (And that doesn't even

> I can't help but wonder about what our brains might have done with all the time we've dedicated to staring at our screens.
>
> —*Juliet, 17*

include the time they spend using computers at school or for homework!)

If you do the math—which is something that the wizards definitely do *not* want you to do—that means that the average American teenager is spending **more than four full months on screens every year.**

That's more than a third of their lives! And if you just count the time that they're *awake,* which is probably around fifteen or sixteen hours a day, then **it's more than *half*!**

TECH WIZARD RECOMMENDED SCHEDULE

9am-11am	Watch videos
12pm-5:30pm	Scroll on social media
7pm-9pm	Play video games

REBEL DAILY AGENDA

- Learn a new song on guitar
- Have lunch with friends
- Bike to library
- Board games with family

CONSIDER THIS:

Imagine you had three extra hours of free time every single day. What could you do or learn? What if your friends had that extra time too?

I could have learned to play the piano, or to tap dance! —*Téa, 19*

TRY THIS! DO THE MATH

Ask one of your parents or older siblings how many months per year they'd like to spend on their smartphone. (Don't be surprised if they look at you strangely and say, "None.") Then ask them to look at the daily screen time statistics on their phone and use the chart on the next page to figure out how many days or months per year this adds up to. How do they react?

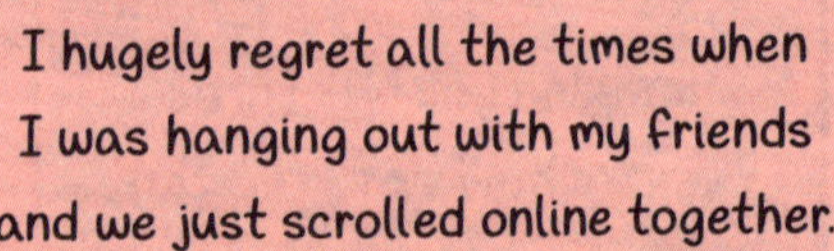

SCREEN TIME CALCULATOR

THAT YOU CAN USE TO

FREAK PEOPLE OUT

1 HOUR per DAY ≈
15 FULL DAYS PER YEAR

2 HOURS per DAY ≈
1 FULL MONTH PER YEAR

4 HOURS per DAY ≈
2 MONTHS PER YEAR

6 HOURS per DAY ≈
3 MONTHS PER YEAR

8 HOURS per DAY ≈
4 MONTHS PER YEAR

10 HOURS per DAY ≈
5 MONTHS PER YEAR

December
ding!
ding!
ding!
ding!
IT'S OFFICIAL! SNOW DAY!
no school! let's goooooo!!!
SNOW DAAAAAYYYYY
BEEP! BEEEP!
Honey!
Guess what!

Meet you at the park?

ding!

ha ha!
whooo!!

click click

heh

em4ever
spent all day in bed
12

The Hidden Costs of Screen Time

A lot of people check their phones constantly because of FOMO, the fear of missing out. But here's the twist: When people constantly check their phones, they miss out on *other* things. These are the **hidden costs** of spending a lot of your moments on screens.

> Between social media and games, there came a point where I felt like someone else was living my life. *—Matthew, 19*

EXPERIENCES

If you allow yourself to be distracted by a smartphone, you may miss out on opportunities for real-life friendship and fun.

> Phones can be "do not disturb" signs to people who might want to get to know you. *—Téa, 19*

This is because **you can't do two things—or be in two places—at the same time.** If you're alone in your room on your phone, you can't also be playing sports or riding your bike.

> With smartphones around, all we end up doing is being on our phones not talking to each other. —*Taylor, 13*

You also can't pay full attention to two things at once. (Don't believe us? Try thinking two thoughts at the same time. It doesn't work.) That means that if you're with a friend, but you also each have a smartphone in your hand or pocket, sending you alerts and notifications, then you can't pay full attention to each other.

PHUBBING

"Phubbing" is short for "phone-snubbing," and it's the name for the annoying experience where someone checks their phone in the middle of a conversation, or is only half paying attention because they're distracted by their phone or are constantly checking notifications on their smartwatch. It feels bad to be "phubbed." But when someone gives you their *full* attention (or you give them yours), it feels really *good.*

MEMORIES

Smartphones also make people miss out on making memories—because you obviously can't remember something if you didn't experience it to begin with! (And you'll remember things better if you pay full attention to them.)

Missing out on memories is an especially big deal for teenagers, because teenage brains are better than adults' brains at locking in memories. In fact, adults' most vivid memories are usually from when they were teenagers.

> If I try to show my friend one thing on social media, we just end up scrolling, and before we know it, it's time for them to leave, and we haven't done anything fun or made any memories. *—Glory, 14*

That means that if you want to have a lot of fun memories of your childhood and teen years when you're an adult, you need to have a lot of real-life adventures and fun *now*.

SLEEP

The CEO of Netflix was once asked who the company's biggest competitors were. You might think he'd have said Amazon or another streaming service. But he said, **"We're competing with sleep."**

This is a big deal, because getting enough sleep is really important! (**Teens need about eight to ten hours of sleep a night**—sometimes even eleven.) When you sleep, your body recovers from the day,

and your brain has a chance to recharge itself and organize all that you've learned so that you can remember it later. Sleep is the closest thing we have to a magic potion; it makes everything better, from your physical abilities to your academic performance to your mood.

But encouraging people to binge-watch shows isn't the only way that screens make people miss out on sleep.

Many screens give off "blue light," which tells your brain it's still daytime and blocks it from releasing a chemical called "melatonin" that helps you fall asleep.

Also, most screen activities—like watching videos, playing games, or texting—are exciting, not calming. That's why many rebels make a point of giving themselves at least one screen-free hour before bed to wind down.

> A few years ago I decided to stop using my phone before I went to bed. Instead, I read for as long as I can before I fall asleep. I think this habit has really made me a happier, smarter person. *—Jakey, 16*

MEET a REBEL

TYLER SMALLWOOD

18 years old, Maryland

Early experiences with tech?

When I was in seventh and eighth grades, I was addicted to video games. I wanted to change, so I started working out. But then I got really into social media and started constantly comparing myself to the people I was seeing online. I was diagnosed with depression.

What helped?

I started actively trying to hang out more with friends in person.

What do you do when you're together?

My friend group's philosophy is to do as many random things together as possible because that's how you create good memories.

What about phones?

When we're out together, we stack them on the table so we can't check them. I can feel myself laughing more and having a better time when we do that.

Biggest piece of advice?

Go do things with people! The more time you spend with friends, the less you'll want to be on your phone.

When I started using social media, I shifted from being a creator to a consumer.
—*Davida, 22*

You won't remember the hours you spent scrolling, but you *will* remember the adventures, the deep conversations, and the times when you were fully present. —*Sophia, 21*

January
We want your talents for the
TALENT SHOW!
JAN 11TH

Hey, David.
Are you going to play piano again?
Wha—!

No, I, um...
I don't really... play in front of people anymore.
That's too bad. I'd love to hear you play.

Anyway, I... gotta go.
Bye.

tk tk tk
tk tk tk
TALENT SHOW
Why did the skateboarder skip school?
He was BOARD!
Er, get it?
"Board" like skate-board, but it sounds like "bored"? B-O-R–

EeeeooOoOO–

–whooAAAaa!!
CRASH
OOF!
clik
At least this'll get more views than the jokes he was making.

Up next is Sophie, who's performing an original song.

clap
clap
clap

strum...

TALENT SHOW

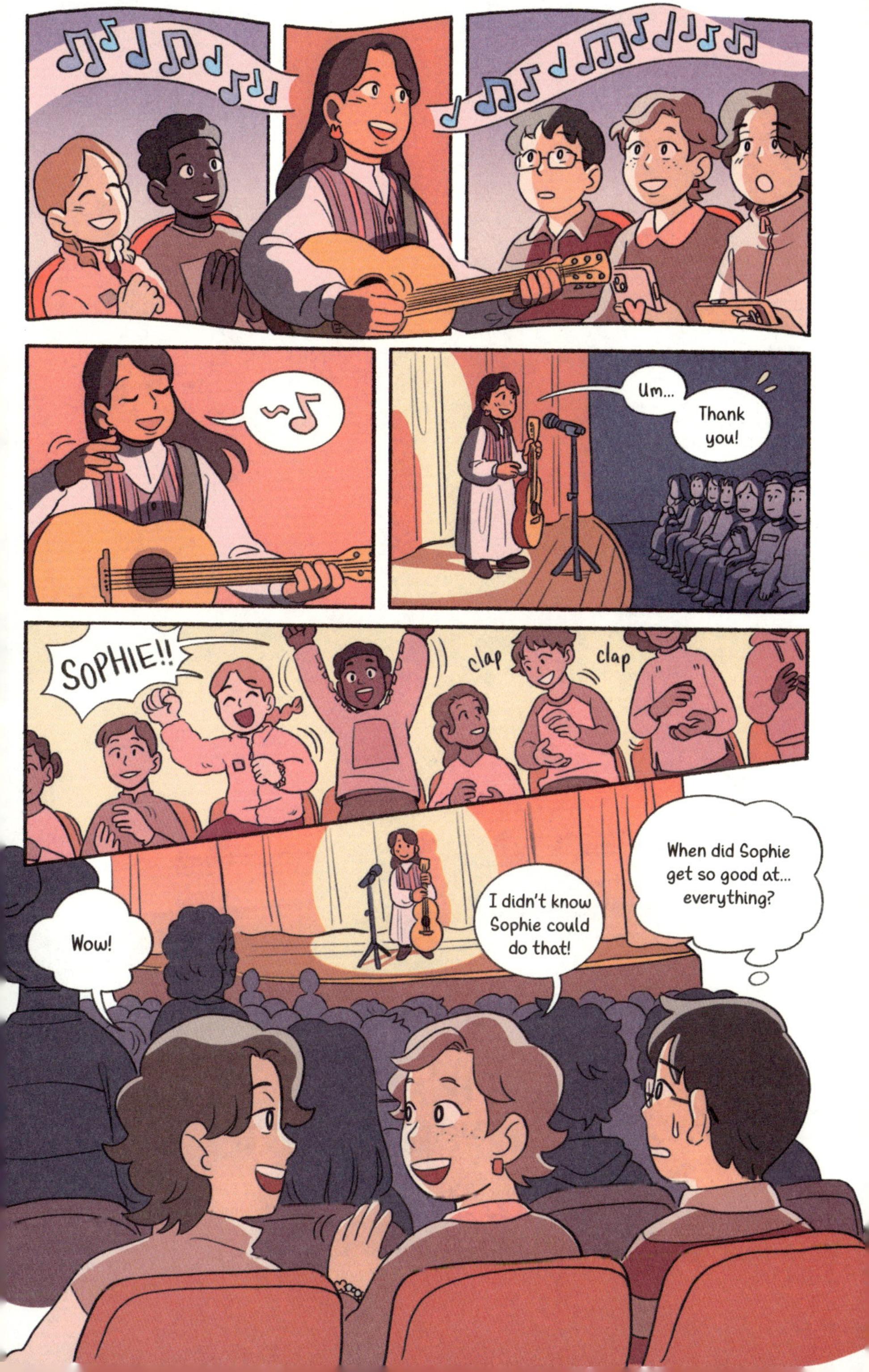

SOPHIE!!

clap

clap

Wow!

I didn't know Sophie could do that!

When did Sophie get so good at... everything?

SECRET #3 The TECH WIZARDS are HACKING your BRAIN

"Hacking" is a word used by computer programmers that means figuring out how to get a computer or program to do something it wasn't supposed to do—like, for example, reveal your passwords.

"Brain hacking" is a term that some tech wizards use to describe how they get *people* to do something that they aren't supposed to do, don't intend to do, and usually don't even *want* to do—like, for example, spend hours a day scrolling on their smartphones and missing out on everything else in life. It works on a subconscious level, meaning a level you're not even aware of, and it's one reason that many people end up spending so much time on apps that they don't even *like*: **Their brains have been hacked!**

If you want to be a rebel, you have to prevent tech wizards from hacking your brain.

Here's what you need to know.

DID YOU KNOW?

Many technology companies have employees whose entire job is to figure out better ways to brain hack people. (They call it "persuasive design.")

Dopamine: The Secret to Brain Hacking

Most brain hacking works by getting our brains to release a chemical called dopamine, which does many things, but there's one in particular that's important to understand:

Dopamine helps us form habits.

Sometimes, dopamine helps form habits that are good for us and that help us survive, like seeking food. For example, imagine you're walking through the woods and you spot a raspberry bush.

Whenever you encounter something your brain thinks might be pleasurable, like ripe raspberries, your brain automatically releases a little bit of dopamine. The dopamine tells your brain, "Pay attention—this could be important." Dopamine also makes you *want* the thing that triggered its release. You see your hand start reaching for a berry, almost as if it's acting on its own.

You pick a raspberry, you eat it, and it's sweet. The pleasure of the sweetness triggers more dopamine, which makes you want more raspberries. It also teaches your brain that it should be on the lookout for more raspberries in the future. Because of dopamine, the *next* time you're in the woods, your brain will automatically start scanning the trail for raspberry bushes, and you may find yourself drawn to the places where you found raspberries in the past—sometimes without even knowing why.

Eating raspberries is a healthy habit. Thank you, dopamine!

But dopamine can also cause us to form habits that *aren't* good for us, such as reaching for a smartphone every time things feel a little awkward or boring, or obsessively checking social media, or playing video games for hours every day. That's because **your brain doesn't *choose* when to release dopamine.** It releases it automatically whenever you come across a dopamine trigger.

Dopamine triggers are things that make your brain release dopamine without you even thinking about it.

How to Design Apps that Hook People

The fact that our brains don't choose when to release dopamine means that it's really easy to design a product or app that gets people hooked: You simply pack it full of dopamine triggers.

The more dopamine triggers you include in your product or app, the more dopamine will be released by people's brains when they use it. The more dopamine their brains release, the more they'll want to use your product, both now and in the future. They'll develop a habit and, if the habit is strong enough, it will feel like an addiction.

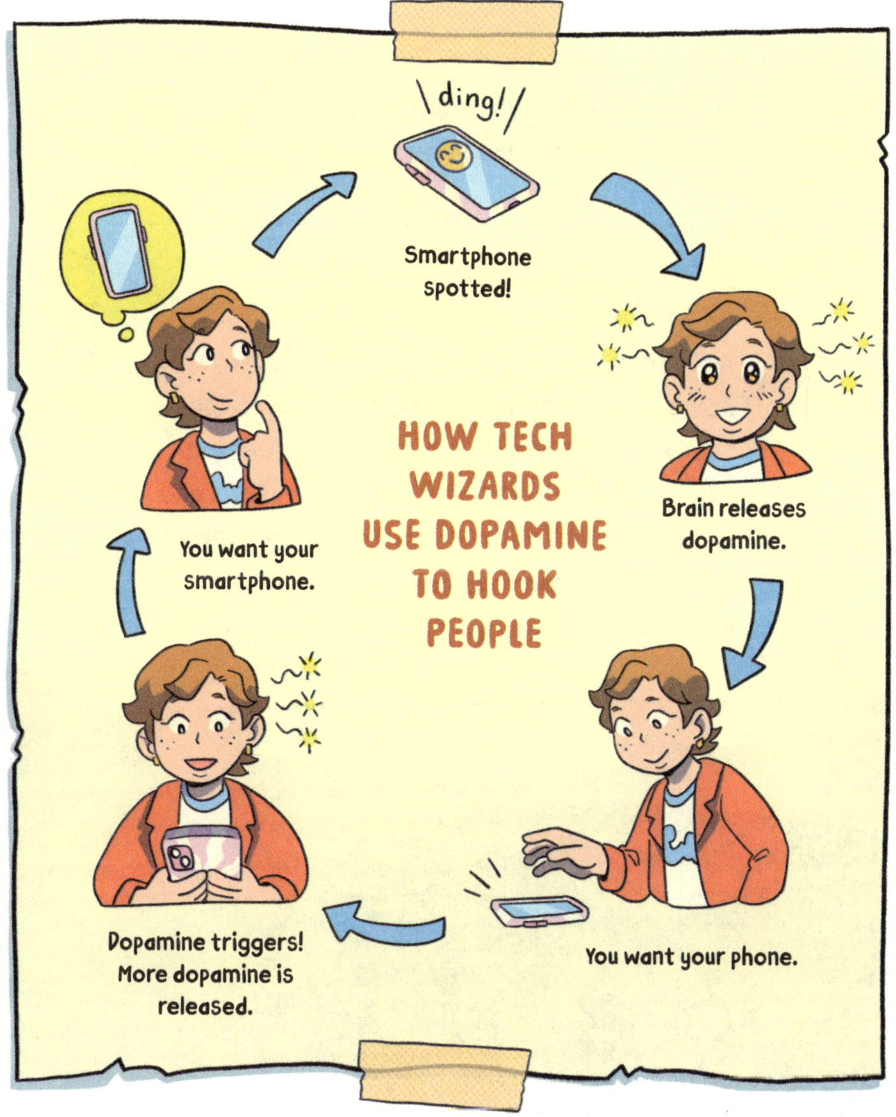

This is exactly what the tech wizards do: **They use dopamine triggers to hook people.** They have even said so publicly:

> *"We need to . . . give you a little dopamine hit every once in a while. [It's] exactly the kind of thing that a hacker like myself would come up with, because you're exploiting a vulnerability in human psychology."*
>
> —Sean Parker, first president of Facebook

WHAT IS AN ADDICTION?

An "addiction" is when someone can't stop doing or consuming something, even though they know it's hurting them or their relationships. You might think of drugs, cigarettes, and alcohol when you think of addiction, but people can get addicted to behaviors too, like gambling and gaming.

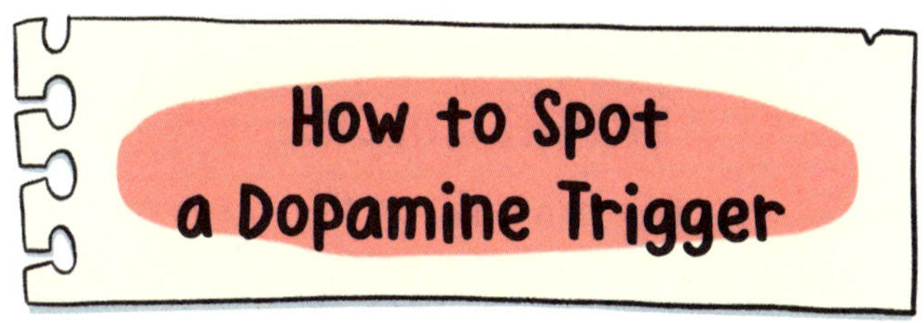

How to Spot a Dopamine Trigger

Here are four of the triggers that the wizards like to use the *most*.

BRIGHT COLORS

NEW STUFF

ding!

ding!

ding!

ding!

ding!

REWARDS

UNPREDICTABILITY

BRIGHT COLORS

As you saw in the example of the raspberry bush, **bright colors are an especially big dopamine trigger.** (See what we did there?) The more eye-catching something is, the more dopamine your brain will release and the more powerfully you'll be drawn to it.

That's why **so many apps are full of bright colors.**

TRY THIS!

Ask a friend or family member if you can turn their screen to black and white. Notice the difference in how it feels to look at the black-and-white screen, compared to full color. (Pro tip: Look up how to adjust the device's settings so they can toggle quickly between color and black and white, instead of having to dig around in the settings every time they—or you—want to switch.)

TRY THIS!

If you have any devices (including a school computer), adjust the notification settings—both on the device and within each app—so that you only receive notifications for things that are truly important to *you*. Turn them off for everything else.

NEW STUFF

Your brain releases dopamine whenever you come across something new, especially if it's surprising. This is why smartphones and apps are designed to show you something new every time you check them: Every new post, video, or notification will trigger your brain to release a little bit of dopamine. And every time that happens, the allure of your phone grows stronger.

REWARDS

Your brain releases dopamine anytime you earn a reward or come across something that *feels* like one. Being rewarded feels good and makes you want to work to get *more rewards*.

> Watching Instagram Reels makes me feel empty. But if I spend time playing guitar, I feel good, because I've actually learned something. —Tyler, 18

This can motivate you to stick with hard things and earn rewards that are meaningful and that really matter to you.

But here's the catch: *Anything* that feels like a reward will get your brain to release dopamine, even if the reward doesn't really matter to you (or anyone else). The tech wizards know this, which is why **they pack lots of opportunities to earn rewards into their apps:** They're using the possibility of rewards to hook you.

In video games, rewards include earning **points or currency, finding a loot box, making it to a new level, discovering a secret feature of the game, or getting higher on the leaderboard.** These rewards (and the possibility of earning more) trigger the release of dopamine, which will make you feel good and

make you want to keep playing the game.

On social media apps, the rewards are often things like **hearts, likes, follower or subscriber counts, or comments.** (These tricks work *especially* well on teenagers, which the tech wizards know and take advantage of.) These rewards will make you want to check the app again and again to see your "score."

> ***"We get rewarded in these short-term signals—hearts, likes, thumbs-up—and we [confuse] that with value . . . [but] what it really is, is fake, brittle popularity that's short-term and that leaves you . . . empty."***
> —Chamath Palihapitiya, former Facebook executive

Our brains also feel rewarded when we find things that make bad feelings go away. That's why people often pick up their phones when they feel stressed, anxious, or upset: They're hoping to find a reward that will make them feel better.

STREAKS = AN ESPECIALLY SNEAKY BRAIN HACK

A *streak* is when you do something—such as opening an app—every day without missing a day. Your score goes up each day you don't miss. But if you skip a day, the streak goes back to zero.

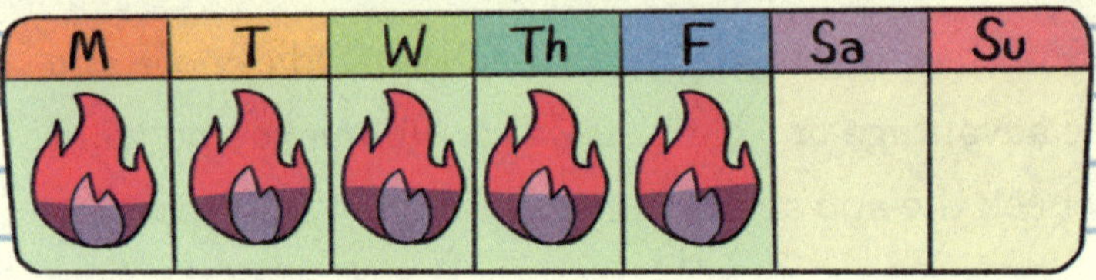

M	T	W	Th	F	Sa	Su

Streaks can encourage you to keep up habits that matter to you, like learning a language or exercising or getting a good night's sleep. But streaks can also be used to get you to do things to help the tech wizards make more money.

For example, Snapchat has a "streak" feature that's specifically designed to get people to use the app every single day, whether they truly want to or not. As a result, some teenagers end up not wanting to go anywhere without internet access out of fear of losing their streaks. Some give their log-in info to friends so that the friends can keep their streaks going for them. Some even pay for the social media company to "restore" their streaks—which of course makes even more money for the wizards.

> Wow, we should add more addicting features like this. —*Snapchat employee, referring to Snapchat streaks soon after the feature was added*

UNPREDICTABILITY

You might think that the best way to train people to constantly check their smartphones would be to make sure there was *always* a reward or something new waiting for them. But the tech wizards know that **the *best* way to train a person—or animal—is to only reward them *some* of the time,** on a seemingly random schedule, so they never know for sure whether they're going to get a "treat." You can use unpredictable rewards to motivate people to do things that are good for them. But you can also use unpredictable rewards to addict them. That's why so many apps deliver notifications on an unpredictable schedule.

The best-known machine that uses unpredictable rewards to addict people is the **slot machine.** A slot machine is a gambling device, often found in casinos, with wheels covered in pictures. You spin the wheels, and if the pictures line up just right, money comes out of the machine while lights flash and bells ring. (These are *all* dopamine triggers.) But you only win occasionally, and you never know if the next spin will be your lucky spin. This unpredictability keeps you playing. Slot machines are so addictive that states don't let anyone under eighteen play them!

Even though kids are not allowed to gamble, the tech wizards studied slot machines when they were designing their own products and built some of the same addicting features into their apps. (This helps explain why they don't let their own kids use them.) In fact, there are so many similarities between slot machines and smartphones that some experts call smartphones **"slot machines that we keep in our pockets."**

TRY THIS! BRAIN HACKING IN THE WILD

The next time you're out in public, notice how many people keep their smartphone on the table when they're eating, and how many people are clutching their phone in their hands while they walk around, even if they have pockets or bags. Bonus points if you can find someone who's been brain hacked into doing something that's obviously dangerous, like crossing the street while texting or looking at their phone as they drive.

THE MORE WORK YOU PUT IN, THE MORE YOU CARE

> There have been games that I've wanted to quit but haven't because of the time I had invested in becoming good at the game. —*Tyler, 18*

Streaks take advantage of another strange quirk of our brains: **The more time or effort we put into something, the more valuable we think it is—even if in reality, we know that it's *not valuable at all.***

For example, if you've spent a lot of time reaching new levels in a video game, or getting a lot of followers on social media, the game or app will feel more valuable to you than it did when you first started using it—and you'll be more reluctant to stop.

When the streak involves another person, as on Snapchat, it's even harder to let it drop because you'll feel like you're letting your friend down. That means the company is using your loyalty to your friend to pressure you to keep spending time on their app.

HOW TO TELL YOU'RE BEING BRAIN HACKED

You constantly have FOMO.

You feel excited but not satisfied.

Real life feels dull.

You lose track of time and feel bad afterward.

You Constantly Have FOMO

If you're constantly consumed by the fear that you might be missing out on things happening online, then chances are you've been brain hacked.

> I feel good when I start scrolling, but when I stop, I feel grumpy, jealous, and lonely. —*Glory, 14*

You Feel Excited, But Not Satisfied

When you're being brain-hacked, it feels like a sugar rush: You get a quick burst of excitement, but this excitement fades fast and leaves you unsatisfied, and sometimes unhappy.

Real Life Feels Dull

The more "sugar rush" excitement you get from screens, the harder it'll be for you to feel excited about anything else, and the more time you'll want to spend on screens.

You Lose Track of Time and Feel Bad Afterward

Many apps are *designed* to make you lose track of time—because the more time you spend, the more money the wizards make. That's why video games have so many levels, and why social media feeds are designed to be endless.

> I would scroll for hours after school and then I'd look up and be like, man, it's six p.m.! I didn't *want* to spend that much time. And now my day's over—and I feel *terrible*. —*Seán, 22*

Spring break

LIVE 301

Oh nooo!

Dude, haha! You went flying!

You've got to pop way sooner.

haha wipeout

omggg

u good? :o

Mom, can you take me to the skatepark? I want to film a new trick.

tk tk

I still have to work today. I can't drive you there.

David, lunch is ready!

tk tk tk

YES!!

WIN

ding!

em4ever

hanging out with ben in london  

 22

Emma, aren't you going to look?

I did, Dad. I took a photo already.

Honey, do you see this–

Oh...

Not **both** of you!

So, anything else you kids need?
Nope, we're all good!
Thanks, Dad!
Um, and then I think this pole attaches there...?
Tent's done!
So's the fire!

Zz...
haha!
haha!

SECRET #4 The TECH WIZARDS are REWIRING your BRAIN

"You don't realize it, but you are being programmed."
—Chamath Palihapitiya, former vice president of user growth at Facebook

Here's something the wizards definitely don't want you to know: **Their products are rewiring your brain.** That's because *anything* you do over and over again changes your brain.

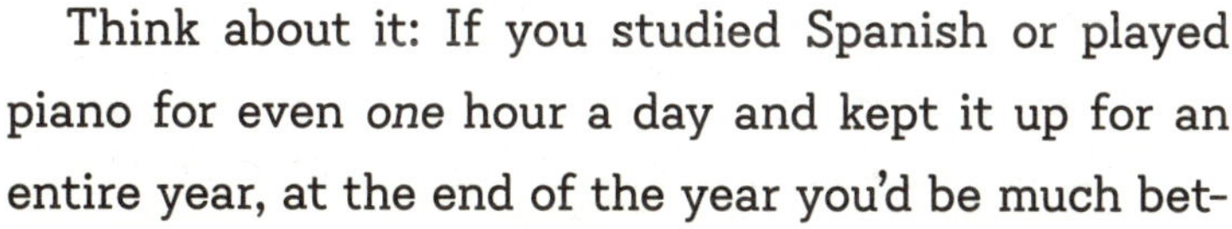

Think about it: If you studied Spanish or played piano for even *one* hour a day and kept it up for an entire year, at the end of the year you'd be much better. That's because when you spend a lot of time doing something, like practicing a skill, your brain creates new connections between brain cells that support

> **Remember:** If you're a preteen or teenager, your brain is rewiring itself right now, faster than it ever will again—and many of these changes will stick around when you're an adult.

the skill and adds a coating that makes those connections stronger and faster.

It's a lot like what happens when you go sledding. The first run down the hill is slow because the snow is fresh and there's no path yet. But after a few runs, the snow gets packed down, the path gets smoother, and you start flying down the hill.

In other words, your daily habits change your brain. That's why rebels regularly ask themselves:

Are my daily habits wiring my brain in ways that help *me*? Or are they helping the tech wizards?

If a habit is helping the tech wizards, then rebels replace it with a habit that helps *them* instead.

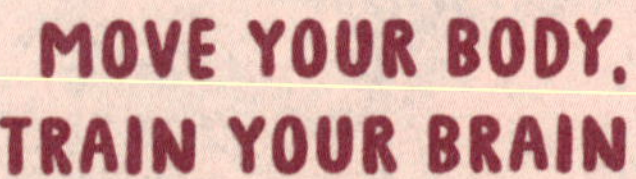

MOVE YOUR BODY, TRAIN YOUR BRAIN

Any activity that gets more blood flowing to your brain—walking, sports, dancing—makes your brain stronger and faster at solving problems. It also puts you in a better mood. Sitting still for long periods of time, on the other hand—which often happens when people are on screens—is really bad for your body *and* your brain.

> Looking back, I feel like the time I spent on smartphones, social media, gaming, and other devices hurt my brain development.
> —*Saiya, 16*

The Tech Wizards Are Damaging Your Attention Span

Our brains are naturally distractible. That's why it can feel hard to stay focused on studying for a test or finishing your homework: **Concentrating for long stretches isn't your brain's natural setting.**

> Spending too much time on gaming and social media has made me a lot less productive and focused. —*Ezra, 18*

For most of human history, being distractible was a *good* thing, because any "distraction" in your surroundings might be a sign of a threat. (For example, a rustling in the bushes could be just the wind . . . or it could be a hungry lion.)

But today, most distractions aren't threats. They're just . . . distractions (often created by a tech wizard who wants you to pay attention to their app). This can be a problem, because the more often you're distracted, the more distractible you'll become. Over time, you'll find it harder to concentrate or focus, and you may find yourself *seeking*

ding!

a distraction anytime things get even the tiniest bit boring or hard.

If you've ever spent a lot of time consuming short, fast-moving content—like **TikTok, Snapchat Spotlight videos, Instagram Reels, or YouTube Shorts**—then you've probably felt this happening: As soon as the video you're watching feels even the tiniest bit boring or slow, you feel an urge to swipe or scroll to something new. If you spend a lot of time consuming this type of content, you'll eventually find it harder to pay attention to conversations with friends and family (let alone finish your homework), since real people (and math!) are usually not as fast-moving and entertaining as a TikTok feed.

DID YOU KNOW?

If you get interrupted while working hard on something, it often can take twenty-five minutes to fully get back on track.

Short-form content completely messes up my mind. *—Sam, 17*

After I got my first smart device, I got really impatient with anything that wasn't moving at the pace of the digital world. Things in the real world got boring or outright irritating to me. *—Gabriela, 23*

HOW TO STRENGTHEN YOUR ATTENTION SPAN

Don't worry if you feel like your attention span has been weakened by social media, video games, or a smartphone. **Your brain is still really flexible!** If you act now, you can undo those changes and rewire your brain for *you*.

Here's an exercise that can help. Choose a time each day (maybe when you wake up or right before bed) to close your eyes and count your breaths—every inhale and exhale counts as one breath. Notice when your mind begins to wander (which it will!), and gently bring your attention back to counting. Your goal is to count to twenty without your mind drifting away to other thoughts.

This may feel impossible at first, but eventually you'll be able to get to twenty breaths. The more you practice, the stronger your attention span will become.

If you find your mind wandering after four breaths, don't say, "Ugh, I only got to four." You noticed that your mind wandered. That's a win! —*Elizabeth Zack, mindfulness teacher*

YOUR RIGHT TO A PHONE-FREE SCHOOL DAY

Most American teenagers who have smartphones report getting more than 230 notifications a day—and nearly 25 percent of them arrive when they're at school.

If you want to be able to concentrate in class (and have more fun at school), you should stand up for your right to have a phone-free school day. A truly phone-free school day means **phones (and smartwatches) are away**—in lockers or pouches, not backpacks or pockets—**from the first bell to the last**, including during class times, lunch, recess, and between classes, so that people talk and hang out instead of scrolling (and no one secretly films you eating lunch).

Imagine walking into a classroom where every student is fully engaged, conversations are real, and there are no glowing screens pulling attention away. —*Khloe, 18*

The Tech Wizards Are Making You Less Creative

The tech wizards like to say that their products help people be creative—for example, TikTok says that the app is meant to "inspire creativity."

But in order to come up with *truly* creative ideas, **your mind needs space and time to wander.** That's why people often come up with new ideas and solutions while they're in the shower or on tech-free walks. By constantly stuffing your brain with new information and content, smartphones and apps leave you with no mental space to come up with ideas of your own. This can leave you *less* creative, not more.

DID YOU KNOW?

The people who make the Oxford English Dictionary chose "brain rot" as 2024's "word of the year." It refers to meaningless junk online that makes you feel like you're "rotting" your brain.

IT'S GOOD TO BE BORED

If you're like most people, you probably hate being bored. But believe it or not, **boredom can also spark creativity.** Why? Because boredom feels so unpleasant that your brain will do anything it can to chase it away, including coming up with new ideas. But smartphones are like anti-boredom machines. With a smartphone in your hand, you never have to be bored—which means your brain will have less of a need to get creative.

"Because of phones, we always have the ability to jump out of ourselves. But unless you learn how to be in your head, you'll never learn how to create."
—Lin-Manuel Miranda, creator of *Hamilton: An American Musical* and composer of music for *Moana* and *Encanto*

The Tech Wizards Are Changing Who You Are

One thing that the tech wizards don't want you to think about is how using their apps for hours a day can change who you *are*.

First, many addictive-by-design apps make their money from ads, and the goal of ads isn't to make you care about who you are on the *inside*. It's to get you to buy stuff. If you spend a lot of time looking at ads—or

SCREEN TIME AND YOUR BODY

Rebels know that all the time people are spending looking down at their phones isn't just rewiring their brains. It's changing their bodies too.

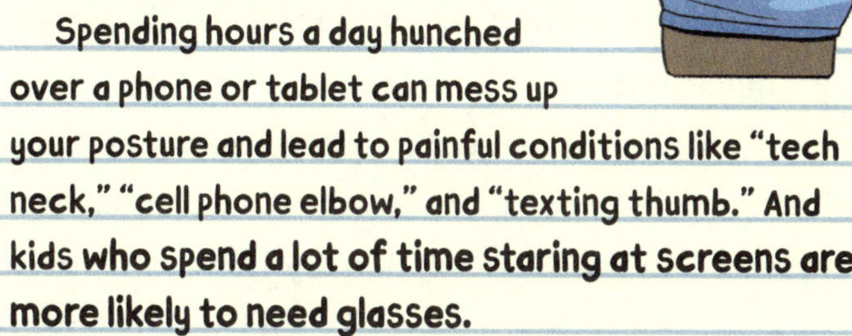

Spending hours a day hunched over a phone or tablet can mess up your posture and lead to painful conditions like "tech neck," "cell phone elbow," and "texting thumb." And kids who spend a lot of time staring at screens are more likely to need glasses.

TRY THIS!

The next time you're out in public, look at the people around you who are hunched over their phones. Does their posture make them look strong, young, and healthy? Or does it remind you of old people?

listening to influencers talk about their favorite products—**you might start caring more about how you look or what you own than about the kind of person you want to be.**

And second, videos and posts put ideas and opinions from other people into your head—people who don't know or care about you personally, and whose main goal is to get more likes, followers, and subscribers (because that's how *they* make money). This might not be a big deal if you only looked at a few posts or videos every once in a while. But if you spend hours every day allowing other people to shove their opinions into your brain, it will leave you with **very little time or space to think for yourself, or figure out who you want to be.**

> [TikTok] defines people my age, dictates our conversations, chooses our outfits, and determines what we buy. *—Juliet, 17*

> I have moments where I wonder: Is this me? Or is this what my phone has made me? *—Bristal, 15*

> If you wait to get social media or a smartphone, you can decide who you are without other people telling you who you should be. *—Calla, 22*

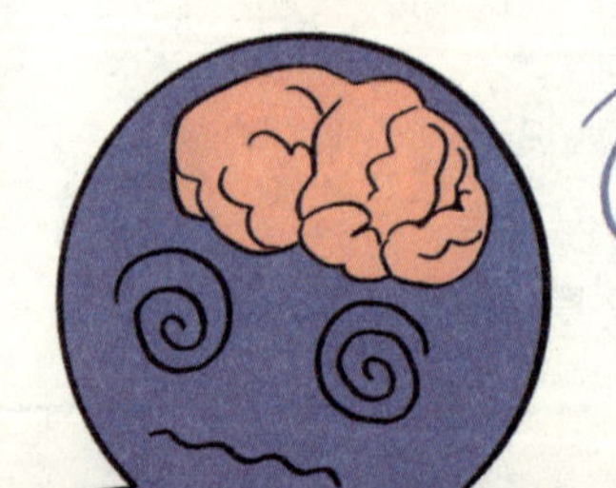

HOW TO WIRE YOUR BRAIN FOR YOU

- **Do you want to be good at concentrating?**
  Do lots of things that require concentration, like reading or playing sports, instruments, or strategic games.

- **Do you want to be more creative?**
  Do lots of things that use your imagination, like drawing, writing stories, or building things.

- **Do you want to be more coordinated?**
  Do lots of things that are physical, like baseball, dance, soccer, hiking, or swimming.

- **Do you want to feel more confident?**
  Do lots of challenging things in real life, like figuring out how to fix things or talking to new people.

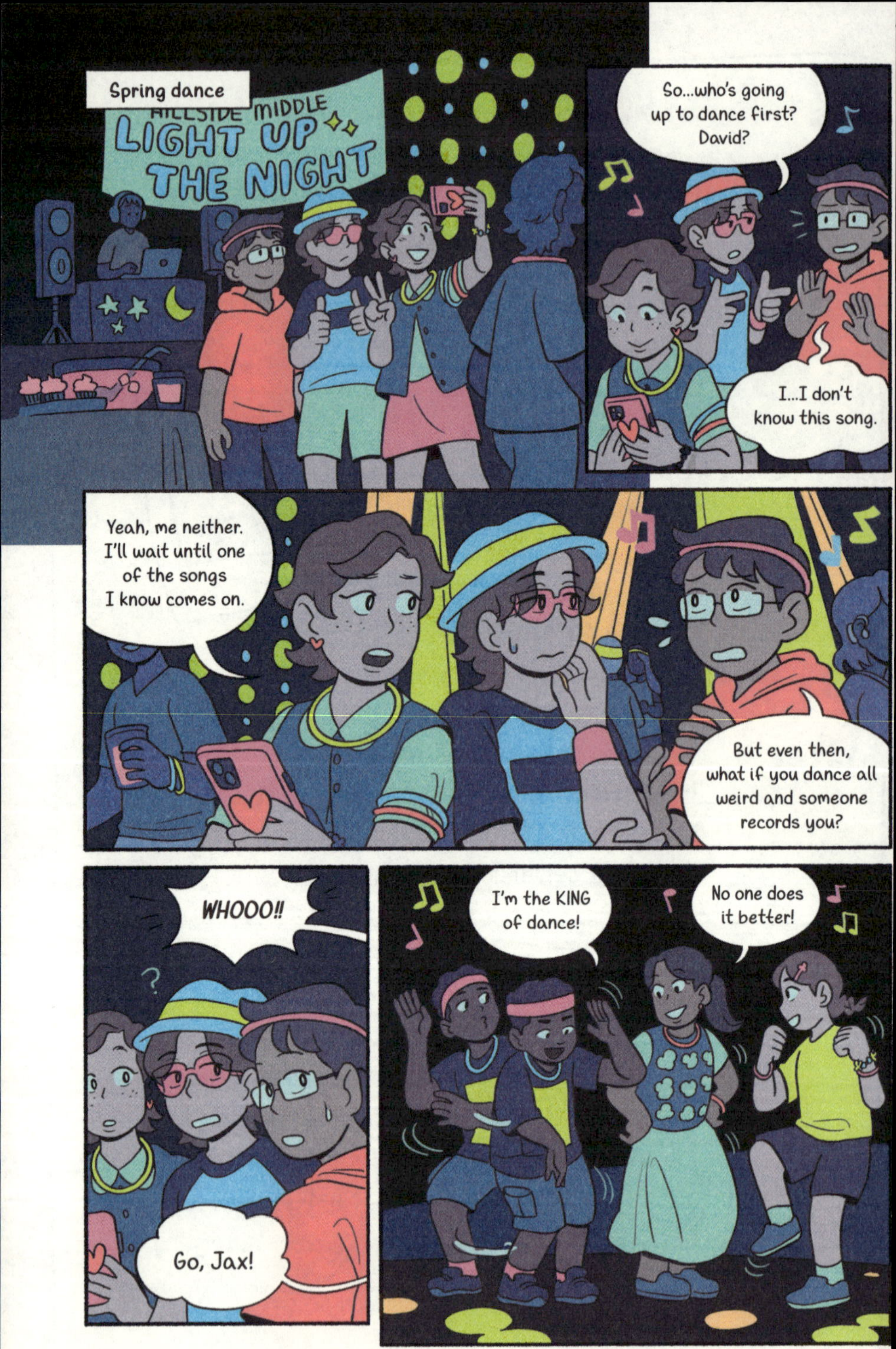

Spring dance

HILLSIDE MIDDLE
LIGHT UP THE NIGHT

So...who's going up to dance first? David?

I...I don't know this song.

Yeah, me neither. I'll wait until one of the songs I know comes on.

But even then, what if you dance all weird and someone records you?

em4ever the dance was sooo much fun! 

♥ 35

SECRET #5
The TECH WIZARDS KNOW their PRODUCTS are HURTING KIDS

In public, tech wizards say that they want to make their products safer. For example, the CEO of Meta posted a statement on his own social media account that said, "It's very important to me that everything we build is safe and good for kids."

But their actions often don't match their words. Instead, the technology wizards protect their *own* kids by keeping them off their products—and **they fight back *hard* anytime someone tries to get them to make changes to protect *other* people's kids.** For example, in 2024 when U.S. lawmakers proposed a bill that would have required tech companies to add more safeguards for kids and teens to their products, the companies spent more than $50 million to fight it.

This is especially upsetting because over the past few years, a lot of secret research documents and private emails have been leaked that discuss **the harms that these products are causing to millions of children and teenagers.**

For example:

- A secret document from Instagram said, **"We make body image issues worse for one in three teen girls."**
- Another secret document from Instagram said, **"Teens told us that they don't like the amount of time they spend on [Instagram].** . . . They often feel 'addicted' and know that what they're seeing is bad for their mental health but feel unable to stop themselves."
- Secret research from TikTok found that **people who used TikTok a lot each day often felt more anxious** and had a harder time thinking and remembering things, having deep conversations, and empathizing with others than people who didn't spend as much time on the app.
- In a lawsuit filed against Roblox, one Roblox employee was quoted saying, "You're supposed to make sure that your users are safe but then the downside [to] . . . limiting users' engagement, [is that] it's hurting our metrics. It's hurting our active users, the time spent on the

platform, and in a lot of cases, the leadership doesn't want that." Translation: Roblox knows it should care about its users, but its leaders don't want to make changes that would make kids spend less time on it.

The technology wizards also know that their platforms are being used by bullies and criminals:

* They know that bullies use social media apps to torment their classmates.
* The companies know that drug dealers sell drugs to teens on their platforms, including fake pills laced with extremely dangerous substances that have killed thousands of teenagers.

> I was bullied by boys in my grade for what I would post. It still affects my confidence to this day. *—Kendall, 22*

* They know that there are many adult men who pretend to be attractive teens online, and then convince a child or teen to send them inappropriate photos of themselves. As soon as a kid sends a photo,

> Strangers on the internet don't always have the best intentions for you.
> *—Anton, 18*

the man threatens to send it to the kid's family and friends unless the kid sends him money. (See page 168 for tips on how to avoid creepy people online.)

DID YOU KNOW?

When a Meta employee asked a coworker what the company was doing to protect kids from some of these bad people, the coworker wrote back that "**Child safety is an explicit non-goal** this [half year.]" That's a fancy way of saying: We're not even *trying* to protect kids.

Is "Big Tech" Just Like "Big Tobacco"?

There's another industry that has spent years keeping secrets, telling lies, and trying to addict young people: the companies that make products containing nicotine, such as cigarettes and vape pens. They're often referred to as **"Big Tobacco,"** just like how the largest technology companies are often referred to as **"Big Tech."**

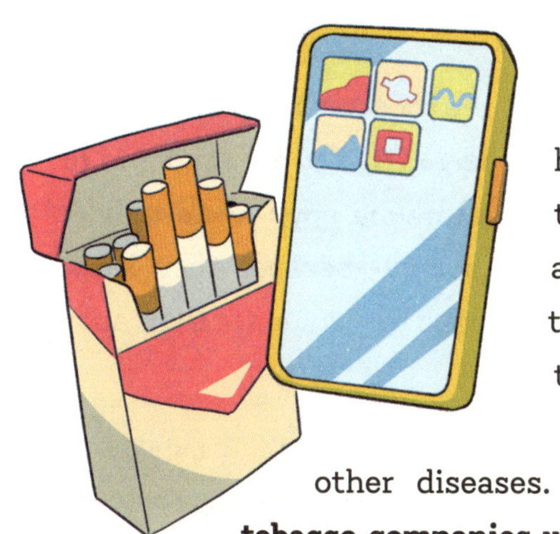

Tobacco companies have spent decades trying to addict kids and teenagers even though they know that their products cause cancer and other diseases. Believe it or not, **tobacco companies used to advertise on cartoon programs and even gave out free cigarettes near schools and playgrounds!**

Tech companies have done similar things: They've created apps specifically for children, like Messenger Kids and YouTube Kids. They give free educational products like Google Classroom to schools (because if kids get accounts when they're young, they're likely to keep using the apps when they're adults). And now they're trying to get AI (artificial intelligence) to be used in schools too, beginning in kindergarten. According to one leaked document, the tech wizards at Meta once even tried to figure out how to use playdates to get more children to sign up for Messenger Kids.

> What made [social media] so addictive was that I just wanted to fit in. . . . I didn't want to be left out. *—Alexis, 20*

What's more, just like the tobacco companies, some **social media companies have tried to get students to sign up for and use social media apps *while they're hanging out together at school***—because they *know* that the best way to get teens to sign up for their apps is to give them FOMO.

> ***"Getting critical mass in a high school very quickly (e.g., in the same afternoon) is extremely important."***
> —secret document from Instagram

The tobacco companies were eventually forced to admit that they knew their products were dangerous and that they had been deliberately lying and trying to addict young people. They had to pay huge fines, and new laws were passed to stop them from targeting kids.

It makes you wonder: **Will something like that ever happen to the tech companies?**

The Tech Wizards Need You More Than You Need Them

The tech wizards want you to think that you and your friends *need* their apps and devices. They've certainly done a good job convincing people that this is true—that's why so many people in the generation above yours grew up feeling like they had to have smartphones and social media accounts when they were teenagers.

But here is perhaps the biggest secret of them all: **It's the wizards who need *you*.**

Think about it: The tech wizards make their money by getting people to spend time on their apps and devices. **If people stopped spending so much time on apps and devices, the tech wizards would make a lot less money.**

That's why the tech wizards are working so hard to keep their secrets. They know that if you and your friends knew the truth—and if your generation rebelled by not using their creations—**their businesses could be destroyed.**

So What *Is* the Truth?

The truth is that despite what they say, **the tech wizards don't care about you as a person. They think of you as a *product*.** They want to drain as much of your time and attention as possible and program you to behave in ways that make you more valuable to their real customers: the companies paying for ads.

"Why do we care about tweens? [Because they] are a valuable but untapped audience."
—private presentation from Facebook

This means that their goals are likely the opposite of what you want for yourself.

- **The tech wizards don't want you to have lots of real-world interests,** because if you did, you'd spend less time playing their games and scrolling on their apps.

- **They don't want you to have fun with your friends** in person, because they want you to look for community online.
- **They don't want you to be able to focus or concentrate,** because the weaker your attention span is, the easier it is for them to distract you.
- **They don't want you to know how many people in the generation above yours regret getting smartphones and social media accounts when they were your age,** because if you did, you might decide not to get them.

Above all, **they don't want you to think for yourself.**

Because if you did, you might decide to **become a rebel and fight back.**

April
So, what subject should we choose for the science fair?
Well, you like biology and stuff, right?
Maybe something to do with animals?
Ooh, maybe an observation of animal behavior.
Like what, in birds or something?
BONK!
OOOOOF!
Yeah...or something.

Later that week
Hey, this weekend we should—
—uh, guys?

Do you mind if I see the screen-time stats from your phone?
It's for a school project.
Sure...?

Hey—
brring!
—on average, how many—
ding!
—notifications would you—
beep!
ding!
ding!
—say you get every hour?
chiirp!

tk—
tk
tk

You guys are going to love this display.

Wednesday, 3:05pm
ALEX
just posted a new vid!
DAVID
nice it turned out good
EMMA
hey any ideas for the science fair project?
Wednesday, 5:36pm
hello???

Wednesday, 6:10pm
DAVID
hm, i looked up some ideas but found this
Video: How to use AI for science fair project!!
ALEX
yesss, this looks too easy
EMMA
i like it lol work smarter, not harder

TODAY!
SCIENCE FAIR
Here's our hypothesis:
Tech companies are manipulating kids into using smartphones in ways that actually make them feel worse.
WHO'S WINNING?
KIDS VS. TECH COMPANIES
Nearly 50% of
The more time you spend on your smart-phone, the more money these companies make.
And so, many apps are made to be as addicting as possible—especially social media!
Nearly 50% of people aged 18 to 27 wish that TikTok, Snapchat, and X had NEVER BEEN INVENTED!
Social media companies act just like cigarette companies: They try to hook kids young!
More than half of 15- to 17-year-olds say that they're online almost constantly.

Every minute you spend on these time-sucking apps is a minute spent making money for those companies...
...and you're not getting paid for it!
How do you want to spend your free time? Making money for other people?
CHOOSE YOUR FUN
VS
Or how about... Reading? Hiking? Spending time with friends?
The average teenager spends more than 8 hours per day on screens
That doesn't include school or homework
HOW MANY DAYS IN A YEAR ARE WE SPENDING ONLINE?
4 hours/day ≈ 60 days/year
6 hours/day ≈ 90 days/year
8 hours/day ≈ 120 days/year
10 hours/day ≈ 150 days/year
That's three and a half months per year—
almost a third of their time ALIVE!
Spending that much time on smartphones and screens also changes your brain—
often in ways that you don't want.
And that can make it harder for you to be successful in other things!

Most American teenagers get MORE THAN 230 notifications per day!
For example, constant notifications.
Those interruptions make it much harder to pay attention and remember things.
ding!
The more time you spend on social media when you're a teenager, the more likely you are to feel anxious and depressed!
HOW TO PROTECT YOUR BRAIN
Smartphones: wait until at least high school
Social media: wait until at least age 16
Plus, if you try too hard to be like people you see online...
you'll miss out on developing your own identity.
So, the choice is yours...
Do you want to live your life for the tech companies?
Or do you want to live for YOURSELF?
IS SCIENCE FAIR?
So what exactly is your project about?
Um...science?

OME BACK
DENTS!
ADVENTURE CLUB!
LESS PHONE = MORE FUN
MORE FUN = LESS PHONE

PART THREE

HOW TO BE A REBEL

CHOOSE YOUR FUN

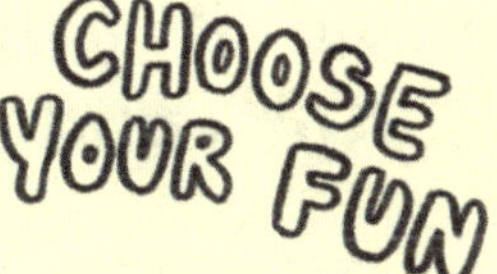

Not following the crowd makes you unique and independent. —Saiya, 16

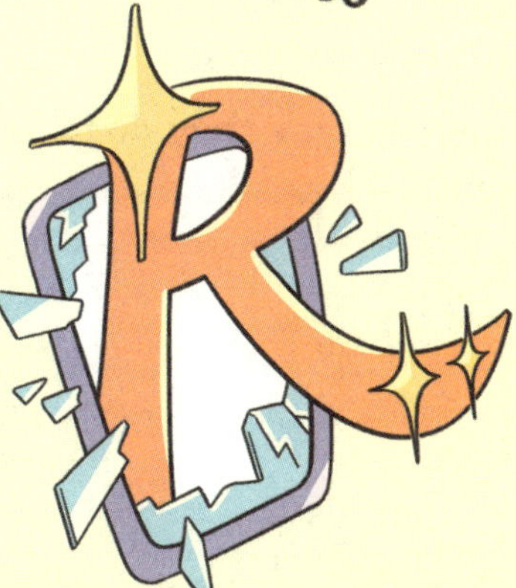

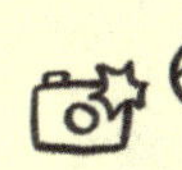

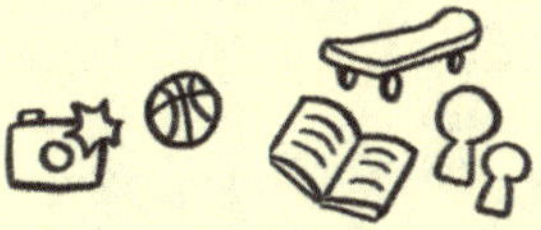

So, what do you think? Do you want to follow the wizards?

Or do you want to be a rebel and choose your own path?

No two rebels are the same, but they all live by two simple principles, known as the Rebels' Code.

THE REBELS' CODE

- Use TECHNOLOGY as a TOOL—DON'T LET technology use YOU
- FILL your LIFE with REAL FRIENDSHIP, FREEDOM, and FUN

Here's how they do it.

How to USE TECH as a TOOL

REBELS PROTECT their BRAINS

The rebels know that the *most* effective way to make sure that they're not being brain hacked by tech wizards is to avoid using their most problematic products, especially until their brains are past their most flexible, vulnerable state.

> **REBEL RECOMMENDATIONS**
>
> - Wait until *at least* high school (if not longer) to get a smartphone.
> - Wait until you're *at least* sixteen (if not older) to open a social media account.

That's why **many rebels wait to get smartphones until they're *at least* in high school (if not older) and choose not to open social media accounts until they're *at least* sixteen**—if they open them at all. It's also why rebels who already have social media accounts sometimes delete or deactivate them, and why rebels who did get smartphones before high school sometimes choose to trade them in for simpler phones.

There's no way for tech wizards to rewire your brain if they don't have access to it.

> I wish I had waited to get a smartphone. I wish I had stayed myself for a little longer. —*Bristal, 15*

PHONES

Not having a smartphone until at least high school might sound difficult, because, well, it *can* be difficult to do, especially if a lot of your friends and classmates already have smartphones. But rebels your age know that the fact that their brains are changing so quickly right now means that **of all the times in life when they could have smartphones, right now would be the *worst*.**

> When I was in middle school, I had a phone that had all the functions of a regular smartphone, but didn't allow you to download social media. It allowed me to enjoy my childhood. —*Sophia, 15*

Some rebels don't have phones at all—either by choice or because their parents won't let them. Others simply **avoid *smart*phones,** with their constant notifications, unlimited internet access, and addictive-by-design apps.

Instead of smartphones, these rebels have **basic phones or smartphone alternatives:** phones that mostly just let them call and text people.

> All my social anxiety went away within about two weeks of getting rid of my smartphone. *—Seán, 22*

There are lots of these basic phones available, and many of them look just like smartphones (but are much cheaper). Each of these phones is different, and many have additional "tool" apps, such as music players or maps. But none include features that give the tech wizards access to your brain, such as unrestricted internet browsers or the ability to download social media, video apps, and games. In other words, **they're designed to be tools, not temptations.**

MEET a REBEL

MIKE SORRELL

15 years old, Texas

What devices do you have?
I have a computer that I use for schoolwork and for texting. I don't have a phone.

Do you want one?
Yes, but I don't think I'm ready for one yet. If I had one, it would consume a lot of my free time.

What's the right time to get a smartphone?
I think kids should wait till they're freshmen or sophomores in high school so their brains have had more time to develop.

What do you notice about your friends who do have smartphones? When we're together and there's a quiet moment, they open their phones and scroll.

Do you have FOMO?
Not really. I don't care about what people post or what they do online. I'll just go out and do something else. I like being seen as someone who doesn't have to do what everyone else does.

Do you feel lonely?
Not at all. I have great friends and a great family—I just don't have a phone.

SOCIAL MEDIA

Rebels know that **opening a social media account is like handing the wizards the key to your brain.** You're basically putting them in charge of how you feel about yourself and how you spend your time. You are giving them a chance to wire your brain for *them*, not you.

What better way to be cool than to fight back against these corporations by staying off the apps?
—Kaylee, 21

For example, **social media apps encourage you to compare yourself to other people** (including strangers). This is likely to make you feel bad about yourself, even if you *know* that the other people are using editing tools to change their appearance, picking photos that make their lives look more exciting than they actually are—or are flat-out lying. Social media also can encourage you to do things (and act fake) just to impress other people.

I would tell my younger self to get off social media apps and go make some memories. *—Tariq, 18*

Rebels also know that they don't *need* social media to be connected with friends and have fun. So **they stay off the apps.**

DID YOU KNOW?

It's **illegal** for social media companies to allow anyone under thirteen to open an account!

Every time I feel good about myself, I go over to Instagram, and then it all goes away. *—Eva, 17*

Social media in particular made me feel awful. Seeing my friends' pictures made me feel like I lived a boring life. *—Matthew, 19*

My decision to delete my social media accounts came from one specific moment. I was sitting in my school's lounge across from someone I had known since I was five. I distinctly remember wanting to reach for my phone to fill the silence instead of talking to him. I could feel the craving in my body; it felt like it was out of my control. A few days later, I decided to delete everything. *—Kate, 24*

People would be like, "Whoa, you don't have *any* socials?" I'd say no, and they'd usually pause for a second, and then instead of judging me, they'd say, "Man, I wish I did that." *—Ben, 22*

Do you have social media but don't feel quite ready to deactivate or delete your account? Turn to page 174.

MEET a REBEL

GABRIELA NGUYEN

23 years old, California

Founder of the "Appstinence Movement"

What is "appstinence"?

It means not having personal social media accounts and choosing to communicate directly with people mostly through phone calls and sometimes texts.

Why did you get rid of your own social media accounts?

I started spending several hours a day on these platforms–before, during, and after school. I was on social media when I was supposed to do other things that I also wanted to do, like spend time with my family, exercise, and do my homework.

What happened?

I tried cutting back and taking breaks, but it didn't work. But once I fully walked away from social media, I found the peace that I had been looking for, and my relationships got better because I had more time and energy for them.

What happens when you meet new people?

They often ask me for my Instagram, TikTok, or Snapchat to stay in touch. I say "Sorry, I don't have any of those–but I can give you my phone number."

How do they react?

They say, "Really? Good for you." Sometimes they add, "I wish I could do that," and I say, "You can."

BE AN INSPIRATION

If you can find even *one* friend who also wants to take a stand against the tech wizards by choosing not to get a smartphone or social media account, you'll double your strength. But **don't be discouraged if at first no one joins you.** If you lead the way, they may follow.

> If you don't get a phone, you're helping your friends fight against the tech companies too. *—Sam, 17*

TIP: BLAME YOUR PARENTS!

If you've decided that you don't want a smartphone or social media account but are worried about how friends and classmates will react, ask your parents if you can "blame" them by telling people that you don't have a smartphone or social media because your parents won't let you.

> People don't want to be on smartphones as much as you think. *—Aralyn, 18*

> It sounds cheesy and stupid, but let your parents protect you. You'll thank them for it later. *—Kate, 24*

How Rebels Stay Connected

One of the wizards' sneakiest tricks is to make people feel that if they don't have smartphones and social media apps, they'll be lonely. But rebels know that a lot of the time, smartphones and social media apps actually make people feel *lonelier*. So they've come up with lots of strategies that help them stay connected with their friends:

> I used to think that smartphones were a way for people to stay connected. I now think smartphones are about 5 percent communication for pressing matters and 95 percent enablers of toxic emotions. *–Calla, 22*

- Whenever possible, **rebels get together in person.** That's by far the most fun option.
- When rebels can't get together in person with their friends, they **call them,** using their own basic phones, their computers, their parents' phones, or their families' landlines. Phone calls are more fun than typing out conversations with your thumbs, and will make you feel closer to your friends. (It's also much easier to read someone's emotions if you hear their voice.)

» **Tip:** Ask your parents to **get a landline** if your family doesn't have one. Tell them that this doesn't require an expensive service plan. There are phones that make calls over the internet using something called **Voice over Internet Protocol** (VoIP for short), and once you've bought the equipment, some of these phones are free to use—forever! Even if your parents say you are too young for a basic phone, they may say yes to a landline since that's what they (or their parents) used when they were kids. (If they don't, ask if you can call your friends on *their* phone.)

» **Video calls** can be good too, unless you notice that you're paying a lot of attention to how you look while you're on the call. (If that happens, go back to regular phone calls.)

- When they just have something quick to say, rebels use **texting** as a fine third option. But they use the phone's built-in message app or a computer, *not* social media—and if too many texts start flying back and forth, they stop texting and just call. They also know that anything they say in a text message can be captured by a screenshot and shared with other people.
  - **Tip:** In order to stay in touch with less rebellious classmates—and avoid missing out on fun plans—**tell your friends and classmates that you don't communicate via social media** and that the best way to get in touch with you is by a phone call or direct text message.

TRY THIS!

Consider going extremely old-school by writing an actual *postcard or letter* to a friend or relative. You may be surprised by how much more fun it is to get a letter in the mail than to get a text message. And it's much more fun to look through old letters than it is to scroll through old texts.

TRY THIS!

Ask your parents or grandparents about whether they had pen pals when they were your age. Did they keep any of their letters? If so, ask them to show you one.

I found a group of friends through skateboarding. When I first joined, everybody was constantly texting and Snapchatting each other for everything. But I started calling everybody instead of texting, and people started to realize how much quicker it was to make plans on the phone instead of over a drawn-out four-hour Snapchat conversation. Eventually, everyone just started calling each other and no one really texted or used social media to interact. *—Seán, 22*

MEET a REBEL

SEÁN KILLINGSWORTH

22 years old, Florida

Founder of the Reconnect Movement

What's Reconnect?

It's a network of clubs for meeting people and doing stuff without phones.

What do people do at Reconnect events?

Sometimes there's a plan, like going on a hike, but mostly, we just hang out. It's not about the event or activity, it's about building a space where people can talk, laugh, and feel like themselves.

What happens when people put away their phones?

The mood instantly changes. Conversations get better. People loosen up. Everything's more fun.

What has becoming a rebel given you?

The ability to make deep and meaningful friendships. The ability to find joy in life. The chance to contribute to something bigger than myself.

Advice for would-be rebels?

Do you want to be another person limited to a phone? Or do you want to open yourself up to experiencing true *adventure*? Trust me, once you get a taste for the connection, excitement, and fun on the other side, you won't want to go back.

How Rebels Deal with FOMO

The idea of not having a smartphone or social media account may spark some intense fear of missing out. That's **exactly the way the wizards have planned it.**

> When I put my phone down, I actually started living. *—Sophia, 21*

But rebels say that taking a stand is worth it.

> I got a smartphone and social media account when I was a young teenager because I was worried about missing out on things. But now that I'm forging my own path, my friends and I have so much more fun. *—Alyssa, 26*

Also, missing out on things online isn't necessarily a bad thing. For example, if you choose not to have a smartphone or social media account, you'll avoid getting sucked into online drama and you'll be less likely to be cyberbullied.

And you won't just avoid bad things; **you'll have more time for good stuff.** As you know, many teenagers are spending five hours on social media every day, which adds up to seventy-five full days a year.

> All the truly gossip-worthy events happen in person. *—Aralyn, 18*

That means that if you and your friends decide *not* to be on these apps, **you'll have an extra two and a half months every year**—that's an entire summer break!—to spend doing other things that you enjoy. That is a *lot* of time.

BEING DIFFERENT

If you're worried that not having social media or a smartphone will make you stand out from everyone else, remember that many people *choose* to be different—for example, by being vegetarians, or by having unusual tastes in clothing or music. Choosing not to have a smartphone or social media account is a similar philosophical choice.

> People are really attracted to people who are different. *—Mia, 19*

And also, according to other rebels, **it may make you stand out in ways that you'll actually *like*.**

> Some of the most interesting and funny people I've met don't use social media. *—Davida, 22*

> You will be more of a mystery to people. That's what I loved about not having social media: Nobody had any idea what I was up to, and would *wonder* about me. *—Freya, 22*

One night...
ding!
?
!!
fwu
mp!
turn

The next day
Emma, are you okay?
What? Yeah. I'm fine.
I've just...
...been getting some...creepy...
messages from some accounts I don't recognize.
Oh my gosh! Really?!
That's awful, have you told your parents?
Are you kidding me?!
SLAM!
They'd just freak out and make me delete my account! NO WAY.
...
Well...what did your other friends say?

People... are NOT nice.
On voice chat, there's always people swearing and saying slurs and other nasty stuff.
Yeah, you should have seen some of the comments I got on my last video.
It makes me never want to skate again.
I'm so sorry, guys. That doesn't sound...
fun.
People can act totally different online.
It's stressful sometimes.
It kind of makes me miss the way things used to be.

REBELS use TECH WISELY

Being a rebel doesn't mean not using *any* technology. It just means being careful and smart about it, and establishing good habits.

THE REBELS' CODE

- **Use TECHNOLOGY as a TOOL—DON'T LET technology use YOU**
- **FILL your LIFE with REAL FRIENDSHIP, FREEDOM, and FUN**

I use my phone like a Swiss Army knife for productivity. **I had to fight to create this type of relationship with it,** but it is better to be in control than to be controlled. *—Mia, 19*

How to Be Smart About Screens and Tech

Not all screens or technologies are created equal. One of the biggest things that makes rebels stand out from other people is that they know how to tell the difference between technology that's likely to hurt or hook them, and technology that can help them and make their lives better.

They do so by asking themselves three questions, inspired by the Rebels' Code:

1. CAN I USE IT AS A HELPFUL TOOL?

If a technology helps you learn, become the kind of person you want to be, or accomplish something that matters to you, then yes: It's a useful tool. For example, if you use AI to explain a math concept that you didn't quite catch in class, or a language app to help you memorize vocabulary words, that's likely a good use of technology. If you watch a great movie, or a documentary that teaches you something, either on your own

DID YOU KNOW?

People have been telling stories for tens of thousands of years, as entertainment and as a way to pass down knowledge about their history, their society, and what's right and wrong. That's why movies, audiobooks, and podcasts are often great uses of technology: They tell you stories and teach you stuff.

or with friends, then that's probably two hours well spent.

But watch out for shortcuts. If you use AI to summarize a book you were supposed to read for class, or to write an essay for you, then you're *not* using tech as a tool to help you—you're using it to get out of hard work. Rebels know that **sometimes it's important to do things yourself precisely *because* they're hard.** That's how you learn and grow.

2. CAN I USE IT TO CREATE *REAL* FRIENDSHIP, FREEDOM, OR FUN?

For example, playing a video game in person with your friends or having a movie night (provided people aren't on their phones) is much more likely to truly be fun

than spending the same amount of time watching TikTok videos, or playing a game alone. Talking on the phone can strengthen your real-life friendships, but chatting with an AI "friend" will not.

3. IS IT DESIGNED TO BE ADDICTIVE?

If so, it's probably best to avoid it.

Also, stay alert for changes that tech companies make to their products that make their "tool" apps addictive. For example, music apps used to just be useful, fun tools that let you listen to music

DID YOU KNOW?

Apps that cost money to use are less likely to be designed to be addictive. For example, Apple Music requires a paid subscription, but it doesn't have the addictive features (or advertisements) that the free versions of apps like Spotify often include.

on the go. But now some music apps have ads and short videos embedded in them (because their creators are trying to compete for your attention with video apps like TikTok). If an app starts trying to hook you, it's time to switch to a different app.

ARTIFICIAL INTELLIGENCE AND FUTURE TECH

The tech wizards are always inventing new things—AI friends, virtual reality headsets, even tech that connects directly to your brain. Most adults don't know how to handle this stuff, and even the people developing AI don't fully understand how it works.

But now you know what to do: Whenever you're faced with a new technology, just ask yourself those three questions (Can I use it as a helpful tool? Can I use it to create *real* friendship, freedom, or fun? Is it designed to be addictive?) and use your answers to decide if and how to use it.

Advice for Other Tech

Here's how rebels handle some of the other most popular technologies, besides smartphones and social media:

WATCHES

"Smart" watches like the Apple Watch *can* be better options than smartphones, but any watch that receives texts and notifications can be extremely distracting too. In fact, watches can be even *more* distracting than phones, because they vibrate on your wrist.

If you get a smartwatch, choose one that can only do a few things, like tell the time, make calls, and send short texts. (And limit notifications, especially when you're in school.) You could also just get a normal watch that you like the look of and that simply tells the time.

WHAT ABOUT E-READERS?

E-readers like Kindles can be great tools, especially when you don't want to carry around a bunch of books. Just be sure to use an actual e-reader, not an e-reader *app* on a tablet (like an iPad) that has a web browser and notifications, so that you're not distracted when you're trying to read.

VIDEO GAMES

Playing video games can be genuinely fun, especially if you play them with your friends, and even more if you can play with friends in the same room. But just like social media, many video games are designed to hook you. If your parents let you play video games, here are rebels' top tips:

> I became literally nocturnal. I'd wake up at five or six p.m., play all night, and go to sleep around nine a.m.
> —*Chris, 28*

* **Watch for Tricks:** Some games use more brain-hacking tricks than others. Make sure you're familiar with the gaming wizards' sneakiest tricks (see page 59) so that you can avoid the games that are the most likely to brain hack you—or be very careful when you play them.

> **TIP:** Don't play games on a smartphone—it's too easy to keep playing everywhere you go. Use a computer or video game console, and don't keep them in your bedroom, because you might be tempted to keep playing when you should be sleeping.

- **Watch the Time:** It's really easy to lose track of time when you're gaming, so set a time limit for yourself when you play. Try not to play more than a few hours a week and to limit your play to two or three days a week, since playing every day is more likely to lead to bad habits and problems.

- **Watch Out for Strangers:** Many video games have chat features that make it possible for adult strangers to contact you (sometimes pretending to be around your age in order to trick you). Instead of using platforms like Discord to communicate, which makes it easy for strangers to message you, call your friends directly using a phone or video calling platform and stay on the call while you play the game—or, even better, **play in person with your friends.** (If you *do* use in-game chat features, set your profile to "private" so strangers can't contact you.)

* **Watch Out for Problems:** About one out of ten players develops what psychiatrists call "Internet Gaming Disorder": They start spending so much time playing video games that it causes problems with their sleep, friendships, performance at school, and/or their family life. It often looks and feels like an addiction: When these players try to stop, they find it very difficult or impossible to do so. If you're worried that your gaming is becoming a problem, ask a trusted adult—like a parent, teacher, therapist, or coach—for help.

TIP: If you feel like you're spending too much time gaming and want to cut back, try taking a three-week break. See "The Rebel Reset" on page 174 for instructions.

> ***"I am very familiar with game addiction, as that's what I thought about every day for more than a decade. . . . [W]e experimented with every feature of our games to see which versions allowed us to extract the most time and money from our players. For us, game addiction was by design."***
>
> —William Siu, cofounder of the mobile gaming developer Storm8

I wish I'd realized that videos and games will always be available, but the chance to be a kid and bond with your siblings and childhood friends doesn't last forever. We all eventually grow up. *—Téa, 19*

YOUTUBE AND VIDEO PLATFORMS

Just like social media platforms, YouTube makes a lot of its money from ads and is designed to suck you in. If you're going to use it, be sure to adjust your settings so that you don't get brain hacked into spending more time watching videos than you mean to, and so that *you* are in charge of what you watch.

- **Turn off autoplay** so that another video doesn't play automatically.
- **Set a time limit** for yourself (and use settings such as "remind me to take a break").
- **Turn off personalized ads.**
- **Subscribe** to the accounts that *you* care about, rather than letting YouTube make suggestions.
- Get in the habit of using the **search bar** to find videos on topics that interest you instead of clicking on recommendations.

- **Avoid YouTube Shorts:** They (and all short-form video content) are especially likely to be "brain rot" and to damage your attention span.
- Remember that just like on social media, **no one is checking** to make sure that the things people say in their videos are *true*.
- **Watch out for influencers who make extreme statements** (for example, they say that all women are like X, or that all people from a particular political party are Y). They're probably being extreme to get more clicks and views (and make more money). Reality is usually more complicated.

How to Protect Yourself from Creepy People Online

Video games often include chat features that let you talk to other players, and many social media apps allow strangers to contact you too. Often they pretend to be teenagers but in fact are much older. They act friendly and they seem totally normal at first, but that's all part of their game. Before long, they may start saying

creepy things, asking for photographs or money, and making threats.

That's why it's extremely important to **avoid chatting with strangers while gaming or using social media.** If you only communicate with people you know in real life, less weird stuff will happen.

Whatever you do, **never send a photograph of yourself** (or, really, of *anything!*) to a stranger online—even if they claim to be your age or send you a photo that they say is of themselves. (It's very easy to fake photos and videos, even voices on the phone.)

If someone asks for photos, tricks you into sending some, or threatens you in any way (including demanding that you send them money or more photographs), **stop talking to them and tell a trusted adult immediately.** Don't feel guilty or ashamed: Millions of people, even grown-ups, have fallen for these lies before. The idea of telling an adult about what's happened (or what you've done) might feel *incredibly* awkward or embarrassing at first, but it will save you from much bigger troubles later on.

Healthy Tech Habits

Rebels know that technology is a part of modern life, and if they want to have healthy relationships with it when they're older, they need to establish some boundaries and healthy habits *now*. Here are some tips for how rebels handle devices of all kinds, including tablets, computers, laptops, and (if and when they have them) smartphones.

MAKE DEVICES LESS TEMPTING

Rebels know how to spot dopamine triggers and they get rid of as many as they can. They turn their devices' screens to black and white (see page 92), delete or hide apps that they know cause them problems, and rearrange their home screens so that they only display "tool" apps, not time wasters. (Some rebels make their home screens totally blank and open apps by searching for them!)

PROTECT YOUR ATTENTION

Rebels guard their brains against distractions by **turning off notifications and using "focus" modes,** which block incoming messages, when they're trying to concentrate. If they need to use a computer for school, they use it just for schoolwork—not to play games or check social media.

Some rebels go a step further and use **app blockers.** These are apps or devices that let you block distracting websites and apps when you're trying to have fun or get stuff done. For example, you could block YouTube and all messaging apps on your computer for an hour so you can finish your homework more quickly—and then go hang out with a friend.

Rebels also create physical boundaries to protect their attention. When they're doing homework, they don't have a device sitting on the table next to them, and they make sure there isn't a TV on in the background.

TRY THIS!

If you have a device of your own, pick one night to do your homework with notifications on. Pick another night to do your homework with notifications off (or focus mode on). Compare how long it takes you to do your homework each night. Is there a difference?

DID YOU KNOW?

The mere presence of a smartphone can be distracting, even if you're not actively using it!

PROTECT YOUR SLEEP

Rebels know that **screens don't belong in bed.** They try to keep devices out of their bedrooms—especially at night—and give themselves at least one screen-free hour before bedtime to help their brains wind down and relax.

They also use standalone **alarm clocks.** Why? Because they know that if they use a device as their alarm clock, it will be the first thing that they look at when they get up—and they don't want to let technology companies control how they start their day.

DO ONE THING AT A TIME

It's possible to watch TV while eating a sandwich, but you can't watch TV while doing your math homework because your brain can only *fully* focus on one thing at a time. Every time it switches between the TV and geometry, it has to slow down a little, like a car making a sharp turn. This is why what adults call "multitasking" will make whatever you're doing take longer—and why rebels make a point of trying to only do one thing at a time.

ASK FOR HELP

Lastly, rebels know that the wizards' companies employ thousands of adults whose *entire job* is to make it hard to stop using their products. That's why some rebels *ask* their parents to set up parental controls or time limits. They know that it's not a fair fight, and that it's okay to ask for help.

The Rebel Reset

When I started reducing my smartphone, social media, and gaming use, I noticed it opened up a lot of space for new hobbies and experiences. —*Saiya, 16*

If you already have a smartphone or social media account—or if you're worried that you're spending too much time playing video games or watching videos—**don't blame yourself.** Remember that many apps, games, and devices are *deliberately designed to be addictive.*

And also, **don't worry:** It's not too late to take back control and reverse any brain changes that may have happened. (Remember: You're young! Your brain is still really flexible!)

Try doing a "rebel reset": **Take a full break for three weeks.**

Be kind to yourself. You're going to have hard days—but those hard days don't define you. —*Tyler, 18*

* **Tell your friends** what you're doing (so that they can hold you accountable) *and* tell them how to communicate with you, so that you don't miss out on fun. (For example, tell them to call you or text you directly instead of using social media.)
* **Delete the app(s) or game(s)** that are causing you problems (or unplug and move your gaming console to someplace inaccessible, like a closet).
* Use the time you've reclaimed **to do or try *other* things** that you're interested in or that sound fun.

Why three weeks? Because when people stop using apps and games that have been designed to addict them, they often feel worse before they feel better. For example, they often feel grumpy, anxious, uneasy, and have trouble sleeping.

This is because their brains have gotten used to unnaturally high levels of dopamine and need some time to readjust to less. That adjustment period tends to last a few weeks, with the first week being the hardest. You'll be going through what's called **"withdrawal,"** and it's the same thing that happens when people stop using addictive drugs. The good news is that, if you can make it through this period of withdrawal, you're likely to feel better—in many cases, a *lot* better. Why? Because **you'll have reset your brain.** You'll also probably find that you've developed some good new habits, or found some new interests, by the end of the three weeks.

Some rebels go through cycles: They realize they're using an app or game too much, they take a break for a while . . . and then the old habit eventually comes back. (If this happens to you, don't beat yourself up. Just repeat the three-week experiment again.) Others simply never go back to their old habits. The spell has been broken.

TIP: When you crave an app or game, try "riding out" the craving like a surfer riding a wave: Try to notice how the craving feels in your mind and body, without giving in to it. You may be surprised by how quickly it passes. (You could also just . . . go do something else! This is a situation where distracting yourself can be *helpful.*)

TRY THIS!

Think of a few fun, easy screen-free activities you can turn to when you crave a screen or need a break, like taking a walk, or shooting hoops, or making something. If your breaks require supplies, keep them nearby. Make it as easy as possible to do these screen-free activities, and as hard as possible to access the app or device that you're trying to take a break from.

The hour after school I might have spent scrolling on my phone is now an hour I have to talk with my family, lie outside, or read a book. *—Kristen, 20*

After I take a break from video games, the urge to play them is gone. I know I *could* . . . but I don't *want* to. *—Tyler, 18*

The last day of school
So we *have* to do a stargazing night sometime. Summer's the perfect time for it.
It's also the perfect time for outdoor concerts.
SUMMER PLANS
-beach
-skate lesson
-stars
-concert
RIIING
Summer break! *Finally!*
My family and I are going to road-trip to the mountains next week.
And then I'm going to volunteer at the nature center.
That's so perfect for you!
My parents agreed I could sign up for skateboarding camp!
I'm *finally* going to learn how to heelflip!
Sophie, you're taking music classes right?
Yep, songwriting lessons! I'm thinking about starting a band next year.

So, um... What are you two up to this summer?
I dunno— probably just hanging out?
My parents signed me up for stuff.
What are you doing, Emma?
I'm still figuring it out.
JULY
What am I doing...?

How to Fill your LIFE with REAL FRIENDSHIP, FREEDOM, and FUN

Rebels don't just avoid technologies that are designed to addict them. They also seek out opportunities for ***real* friendship, freedom, and fun.** Why? Because they know that the more they fill their lives with *real* friendship, freedom, and fun, the more amazing they will feel—and the less they'll *want* to spend time on screens.

DID YOU KNOW?

No one feels amazing—or happy—all the time. But the more your life is filled with real friendship, freedom, and fun, the easier it will be to get through rough patches.

Friendship

Humans need friends in order to be happy and healthy. In fact, researchers have found that feeling disconnected from other people can be just as bad for your health as smoking cigarettes.

Tech companies would like you to believe that you can satisfy your need for friendship with their products. And sure, smartphones, social media, and video games *can* help people connect. But as the generation above yours learned the hard way, a lot of what the companies try to pass off as "friendship" is actually fake.

REAL FRIENDS VERSUS FAKE FRIENDS

A *real* friend is someone who knows and cares about you—the *real* you. They make you feel good when you're together, cheer you up when you're feeling down, and stick with you when things are tough.

When I'm with my friends, I feel overjoyed.
—*Glory, 14*

You trust each other and laugh together. You're able to talk about things that go beyond whatever is trending online.

Friendships would be stronger without social media.
—*Ruqayah, 16*

A **fake friend,** on the other hand, is someone who doesn't know or care about the real you, who makes you feel insecure or anxious, or who disappears in hard moments. A follower is not the same thing as a friend. Neither is an AI chatbot, because a real friend has to . . . actually exist.

DID YOU KNOW?

The CEO of Meta said that he wants to add more AI chatbots to his company's apps to make people feel like they have more friends. This is the **ultimate tech wizard move:** First you cause a problem with one of your products (for example, by making people feel lonely). Then you offer to solve it with another product: a "friend" who is literally a computer program!

Freedom

The technology wizards want you and your friends to think that getting a smartphone is a sign of freedom and independence. But do smartphones *really* make people more free?

REAL FREEDOM VERSUS FAKE FREEDOM

***Real* freedom** is when you feel like you're in charge of your life and you feel comfortable being yourself. It allows you to follow your curiosity, try new things, take risks, mess up, and figure things out—without always worrying that people will judge or shame you.

Fake freedom is when you *think* you're free, but someone—or some*thing*—else is controlling your choices. (Like, for example, an influencer or tech wizard.) You may find yourself feeling pressured to do things that you don't want to do, acting in ways that don't reflect who you truly are, or *not* doing things

Getting a phone and spending all your time on it isn't real freedom. That's being controlled by your phone. *—Ben, 22*

because you're worried about being laughed at or judged.

That's why rebels make a point to regularly try doing things on their own, *without* the internet or a device. For example, can you learn a new skill from a person instead of a video? Can you entertain yourself for an hour after school or make it through an awkward or boring moment without reaching for a screen?

Smartphones prevent me from being able to fully let go and be myself around friends.
—Sophia, 21

CONSIDER THIS

If you were at a party where everyone had their phones out, would you feel comfortable dancing or goofing around—or would you hold back, worried someone might record you and post it online?

Tech companies love to say that their products are fun. But there's a huge difference between the *real* fun you have when you do things in real life (especially with friends), and the *fake* "fun" that tends to happen when you spend time alone on screens.

REAL FUN VERSUS FAKE FUN

Real fun makes you feel great while it's happening, and it leaves you happy, full of energy, and with vivid memories. It usually happens when people are **doing things together in real life**—it almost *never* happens when people are online and alone. (This is true even for introverts: people who usually enjoy being alone or in small groups.) It also doesn't happen when you do something just so that you can post it online. When people have

real fun, their guard is down, and they're being their truest, most authentic selves. **Real fun fills you up, and leaves you feeling *great*.**

***Fake* fun,** on the other hand, is the feeling you get from doing things that companies (or other people) *tell* you are fun, but that don't leave you feeling happy and full of energy. Fake fun often feels exciting at first, like a sugar rush, but **it leaves you unsatisfied.** (It's often a sign that you're being brain hacked.) People rarely remember fake fun once it's over.

CAN PLAYING VIDEO GAMES BE REAL FUN?

If you're playing a game with friends—ideally together in the same room—and if you're all laughing and are totally engaged, then yes!

For most people, the top sources of fake fun in their lives are social media, playing video games alone, and binge-watching TV or online videos (especially short ones). Sure, stuff you see online might entertain you or make you laugh. But if you tried to remember the reels you watched yesterday, you'd probably have trouble. They all become one big blur of distraction.

DID YOU KNOW?

There are also lots of fun things you can do on your own that can recharge your batteries and make you feel good—like watching a movie, reading, exercising, or listening to music. Just get in the habit of asking yourself how you feel after you spend time doing something. If you feel good, it was probably a good use of your time.

TRY THIS!

Keep an eye out for commercials peddling smartphones and apps. Notice how much fun the people in those ads seem to be having. Then find someone in real life who's staring at their phone. Do they look as happy as the people in those ads?

WHAT'S ONE OF YOUR MOST FUN MEMORIES? WHAT WERE YOU DOING? WHO WERE YOU WITH?

Falling in love with someone who also didn't have social media. *—Kate, 24*

Spontaneously going into the city with friends, sometimes without even telling our parents. It felt like we were living a movie, experiencing the kind of adventures people now watch on Netflix. *—Davida, 22*

Dancing on a rooftop in the rain at a concert. Singing and harmonizing with my friends after a long day out in the summer sun. Playing card games all night long. Hiking! Camping! Being outside! *—Kendall, 22*

A friend's grandpa invited me and some friends to spend a week together in a cabin. We explored the woods, we went for night hikes, we rode ATVs, we did polar plunges, we cooked steaks over a fire. It was such an incredible bonding experience. *—Seán, 22*

DO THINGS THAT MATTER

In addition to friendship, freedom, and fun, there's another ingredient that makes people feel amazing: **doing things that matter.** Think about something that made you feel helpful or proud, like doing a favor for a neighbor or teaching your little brother how to tie his shoes. **The more you do things that help other people, strengthen your relationships, or make the world better, the more amazing you will feel.**

So how, exactly, do rebels fill their lives with real friendship, freedom, and fun?

They train their brains to be in discover mode, and they do lots of things with other people in real life.

Summer break
Today was so cool!
click
Hey, Call—!
...
Oh!

Uh, are you taking algebra summer classes here too?

Actually... I'm taking a songwriting class.

I'm having a lot of fun. Maybe you could take it too?
Oh, um...

CHORD PROGRESSIONS
That... sounds cool.
I'll think about it.

ha

I'm heading out now!

Are you sure you want to delete your account?
YES
NO

press
to delete your account?
YES
NO

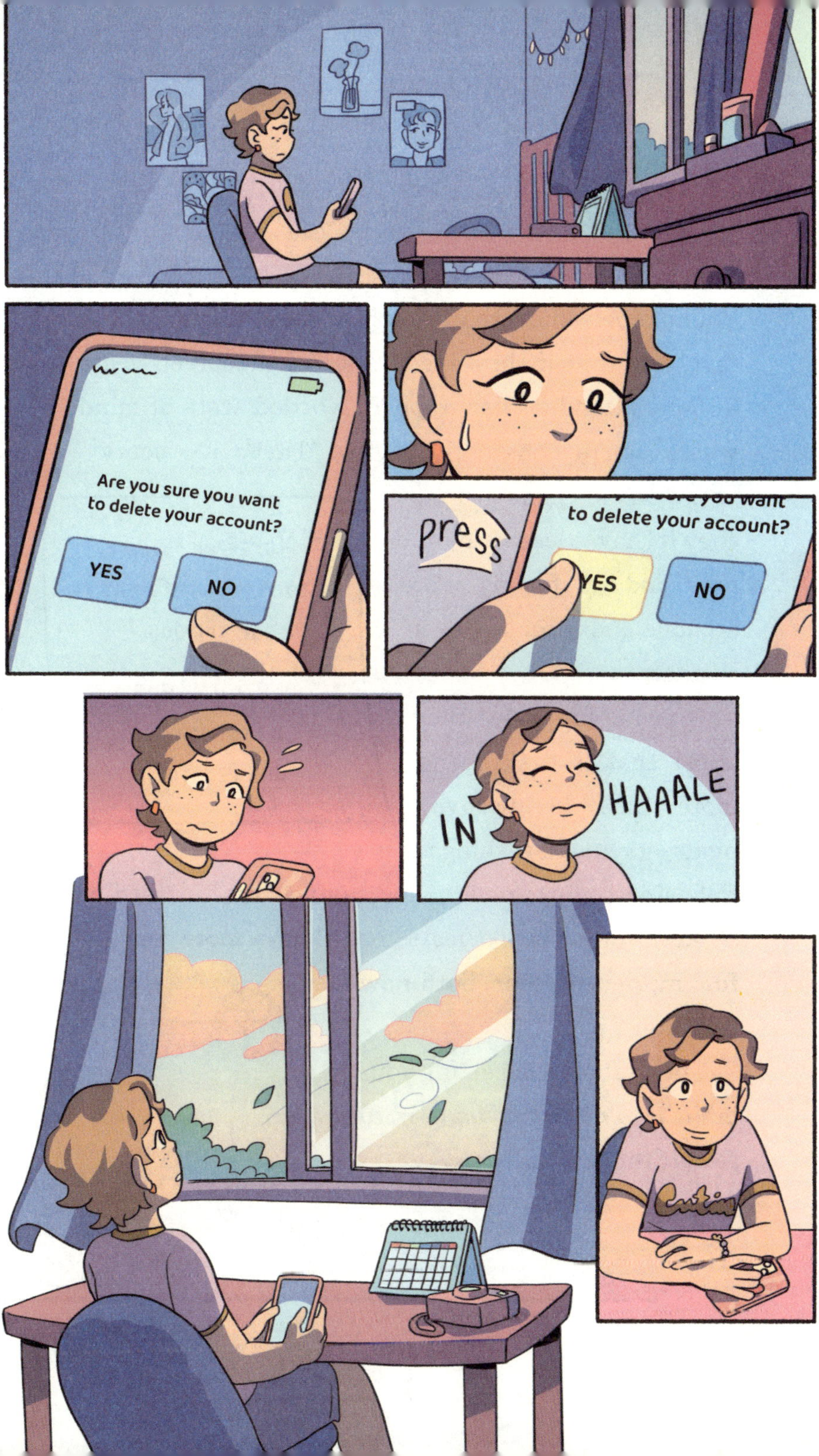

IN HAAALE

REBELS LIVE in DISCOVER MODE

Young rebels know that their brains are changing very fast, and that if they spend a lot of their teen years in defend mode—that trapped, worried state of mind where you're constantly saying "That's too scary" or "What if I screw up?"—they'll have less fun and may end up feeling more anxious and insecure, even as adults.

Discover Mode = You feel confident and curious.

Defend Mode = You feel anxious and fearful.

On the flip side, they know that if they spend more time in discover mode—trying new things, following their curiosity, and saying "Yes" instead of "Yikes!" (or yikes *and* yes)—**they'll have more fun and feel more confident,** both now *and* later.

The first step in getting your brain *into* discover mode is to get *off* the couch. Then . . .

GET CURIOUS ABOUT YOURSELF

One way that rebels train their brains to be in discover mode is to make a point of being curious about **who they are and what kind of person they want to be.** In other words, **they get into discover mode—about themselves.** This is essential because as you know, tech companies are hoping to shape your behaviors and personality in ways that help them make more money. If *you* don't know who you are—or what kind of person you want to be—they'd be happy to make those decisions for you.

Figuring out who you are and who you want to be is a long process (in fact, it's part of what being a teenager is all about)—and the best way to do it is to get out in the world and try lots of stuff. But it can also help to ask yourself some questions. For example:

- Who are a few people you love spending time with? What makes them fun or interesting to be around?

I love going to the trampoline park, swimming pool, and doing stuff outside of the house.
—*Taylor, 13*

- Think of a person you look up to *in real life*—maybe a family member, teacher, coach, or older sibling or friend. **What do you like and admire about them?**
- **What do you want people to like and admire about you?**
- **What are some things you really love doing in your free time?** (For example: playing cards, baking brownies, riding your bike, hanging out with friends.)
- **What's something new you're interested in doing or trying** (like acting, learning to play drums, or crocheting)**?**
- **What's something you've done or tried that you want to be better at?**
- **What matters to you?** (For example: helping people, making the world better, being a good friend.)

TIP: Write your answers down in a notebook or journal so that you can look back on them later. And don't worry if you don't have all the answers yet—you're not supposed to!

PAY ATTENTION TO WHAT YOU'RE PAYING ATTENTION TO

If you want to spend more time in discover mode, you need to pay attention to the things you're paying attention to. Why? Because if *you* don't choose how to spend your time and attention, the tech companies will brain hack you into spending it in ways that just help them make money. So get in the habit of asking yourself:

- What am I paying attention to right now?
- Is this what I want to be paying attention to?

For example, let's say you're hanging out with a friend and you notice you keep worrying about how you did on last week's history test. That means you're in defend mode. You can now *choose* to flip back to discover mode by shifting your attention back to your friend. (Yes, you can actually choose what you pay attention to–at least some of the time.) The fact that you *noticed* where your attention had drifted gives you the power to bring it back–and to direct it toward something you *want* to pay attention to.

5-4-3-2-1

This is another great way to flip your brain from defend to discover mode (not to mention strengthen your attention span and deal with moments of anxiety or boredom). Tune in to your senses and silently:

* Name five things you can see. (For example, "I see a woman in a red hat. I see a dog sniffing a tree.")
* Notice four things you can feel, like the chair you're sitting on, the texture of your clothing, or the feeling of a breeze on your skin.
* Listen for three sounds.
* Identify two smells.
* Focus on one taste.

> Embracing boredom has really improved my well-being.
> —*Saiya, 16*

TRY THIS! PRACTICE DOING NOTHING

The next time you're waiting for something or someone, or are stuck in a bus or car with nothing to do, see if you can figure out a way to *enjoy* having a quiet moment to yourself.

ASK YOUR PARENTS AND TEACHERS TO "LET GROW"

Here's a simple way to flip your brain into discover mode and make life feel more exciting and fun: **Try "The Let Grow Experience."** It's a project that you can ask your parents to let you do, or even ask your teachers to assign to your whole class.

> **The Let Grow Experience:**
> **Try something new—*with* your parents' permission, but *without* your parents.**

Here's how it works:

1. **You pick a new, real-world thing to try on your own.** It should be something you've never done without supervision before, maybe even something that feels hard, or makes you a little nervous. You can do it alone or with a friend or sibling—just not with an adult. This can be a new thing that sounds fun or interesting to you personally, or something that would help your family—or both.

   For example, you could:

   - Play or hang out outside with friends, unsupervised
   - Walk or bike to school or a friend's house

- Go into a store or restaurant to pick up something while your parents wait outside or in the car
- Run some errands entirely on your own
- Strike up a conversation with someone new
- Start making your own breakfast and/or lunch
- Do a favor for a neighbor
- Cook a meal for your parents, maybe with a friend or sibling
- Learn how to fix something
- Mow the lawn
- Taking public transportation
- Earn money by shoveling snow, raking leaves, babysitting, or washing cars for neighbors

For more ideas of things you could do, visit LetGrow.org. (Have your parents and teachers visit too.)

I spent most of my childhood outside, playing and trying new things, getting scraped up, and dealing with it myself instead of running to my parents. It was the best possible way I could have grown up. *—Mia, 19*

The "real world" part is important because real-world accomplishments usually feel better (and are more fun) than rewards on screens. For example, if you learn to bake a cake, you get to *eat* the cake—not just watch a video of someone else eating a cake. If you learn to get around your neighborhood on your own, you'll be able to knock on friends' doors and hang out together. If you run a real lemonade stand, you can earn real money that you can use to buy and do stuff.

TIP:

As you go about your day, keep an eye out for small things that delight you or make you laugh. This is an easy way to encourage your brain to stay in discover mode.

2. **Make a simple plan.** Talk with your parents about what you'll do and how you'll handle any surprises.

3. **Do it (without your parents)!** Being a little nervous at first is totally normal. But you're likely to be surprised by how much more confident you feel afterward. That's the

> Make new friends, introduce yourself to strangers, bake for yourself, learn a new hobby, become a dog sitter. Try out cool things! *—Tariq, 18*

beauty of it: The more new things you do, the less anxious you'll feel about trying *other* new things (even if things didn't go perfectly). And the more things you learn how to do on your own (and the more opportunities you have to bounce back from mistakes and failures), the more independent you will feel—because *you will be more independent.*

TIP: If you want to try something new out of the house but your parents don't want to let you, precisely *because* you don't have your own phone, suggest that they get a "loaner" phone for the family: a basic phone that doesn't belong to anyone in particular that you and your siblings can borrow when you're out of the house–and give back when you're done.

Try adding a new experience every week or month. When possible, do it with a friend. Even if your parents are hesitant at first, once you prove you can handle more independence and responsibility, they'll be more open next time. (And they'll probably *love* it if you take on some of the things they used to have to handle themselves!)

> If you can do one hard thing, you can do another.
> —*Tyler, 18*

REBELS DO HARD THINGS:

Rebels know that trying new, hard things will help them grow and get stronger—even if they fail—and that the most satisfying accomplishments in life are the ones that take work.

WORRIED GROWN-UPS?

If your parents are worried "something bad" could happen if you leave the house by yourself, let them know that despite scary news headlines, rates of violent crime have fallen dramatically in the United States since the 1990s. Given all the risks that exist for kids online, it's usually safer to do stuff outside the house than to be alone in your room chatting with strangers on social media or in a video game.

You can also point out that trying new things builds confidence and self-esteem, and that *not* letting you do anything on your own has risks too: How are you ever going to leave home, get a job, and live on your own if you've never practiced doing basic things like laundry, grocery shopping, cooking, cleaning, and finding your way? Tell them that even small things like walking to a store or babysitting a sibling teach responsibility and problem-solving in ways no screen can.

REBELS do things with OTHER PEOPLE in REAL LIFE

If you've ever been forced to sit through an online class during a virtual school day, you know that spending time with people online just doesn't feel the same as being together in person.

> The best moments happen away from screens.
> —*Nick, 22*

That's why rebels make a point to spend lots of time **hanging out and doing stuff with their friends in person:** It's the best way to fill their lives with *real* friendship, freedom, and fun.

FIND YOUR PEOPLE

Scientists have discovered that having a few *good* friends is more important than having a *lot* of friends. So **try not to worry about how *many* friends you have**—even just one good one is enough.

How can you find *new* real-life friends if you want some? Look for classmates or teammates who have similar interests, who make you feel like you can be yourself, or who make you laugh.

Join a club!
—Bristal, 15

Look for friends who like to go out and *do* things.
—Tyler, 18

TRY THIS!

Pick someone in your class whom you are friendly with, but are not yet close friends with, and invite them to do something, even something as simple as sitting together at lunch.

TIP: **Get in the habit of carrying around a book, sketchbook, or journal. Not only will this give you something screen-free to do when you're waiting for things, but it will identify you as a rebel and help you find new like-minded friends.**

Do activities that make you happy. You'll find people who value you for who you are. *—Saiya, 16*

FIND YOUR FUN

Once you've found your people, the next step is to **figure out things you want to *do***—either with those people, or on your own.

Why with other people? Because doing stuff with friends is fun!

Why on your own? Because it's not always possible to get together with other people, and you might be someone who *prefers* to spend time alone.

Also, **the more real-life hobbies and skills you have, the easier it will be to have real fun,** either on your own or with your friends.

So grab a notebook or a friend—or both!—and come up with a list of things you like doing or that you're interested in trying, *just for the fun of it*, either on your own or with other people.

Here are some ideas to get you started.

WAYS TO HAVE FUN WITHOUT A PHONE

Toss a Frisbee * Learn how to juggle * Explore someplace new * Learn an instrument * Start a band * Go camping * Learn a martial art * Learn to sew * Fix something * Build something * Draw * Paint * Play catch * Read a book * Learn to swim * Learn how something works * Go bowling * Volunteer * Learn how to cook something * Try a new food * Ride a bike

* Send a postcard * Do a favor * Knit a scarf * Build a fort * Redesign your room * Join a club * Start a club * Have a movie night (with popcorn!) * Host a sleepover * Keep a journal * Get a camera * Stargaze * Go for a walk * Make up a dance * Do karaoke * Do a puzzle * Play a game * Make a scrapbook * Start a newsletter * Stare at the clouds * Identify birds * Help a neighbor * Have a picnic * Go ice skating * Fly a kite * Learn origami * Make your own jewelry * Play with a dog * Make a time capsule * Learn how to solve a Rubik's Cube * Do something nice for a friend * Write a story * Learn how to play chess * Learn a yo-yo trick * Have a

paper airplane contest * Wake up early and watch the sun rise * Read a biography of someone amazing * Try a new sport * Go for a hike * Run a lemonade stand * Bake cookies * Make a friendship bracelet * Introduce yourself to someone new * Go fishing * Skip stones * Write a thank-you note to someone important in your life * Have a cookout * Learn the history of your town * Listen to new music * Learn to whittle * Climb a tree * Set up a hammock * Make your parents breakfast * Put on a play * Try out for something * Learn how to do a handstand * Write a poem * Write a song * Learn a magic trick * Learn how to make balloon animals * Invent something

TIP:
GO OUTSIDE

Ever notice how different you feel after spending time outside compared to being cooped up indoors? Scientists have found that spending time outside—especially in nature—makes people happier and less anxious. Whenever possible, do stuff with friends *outside*.

Pro Tips for Having More Fun

MAKE FUN EASY

Rebels know that one of the main reasons people spend so much of their free time on screens is that it's easy. So they make real fun even easier!

Leave your guitar out, keep a book in your bag, or carry a deck of cards. Put out games when friends or family visit, and have a journal, book, or craft project by your bed. Keep a Frisbee or baseball glove or basketball or soccer ball near the door. **Make it simple to do what you love—and harder to get distracted by screens.**

> There's a whole world of possibilities if you take the time to look for them. —*Aidan, 14*

LIVE YOUR LIFE—DON'T PERFORM IT

When people start spending a lot of time creating content to post on social media and YouTube, they often stop doing things just for fun, and start doing them to impress other people. In other words, they start performing

their lives for an imaginary audience instead of living their lives for themselves. This is one reason that **many rebels choose not to open social media accounts or post videos online.**

I think doing stuff just for social media is embarrassing.
—Sam, 17

TRY THIS!

Get into the habit of regularly asking yourself: Am I doing this for me or someone I care about? Or am I doing it to show off or impress someone else?

DON'T BE AFRAID TO LOOK WEIRD

Rebels know that if you're trying something new, there is always a chance that you will fail, perhaps spectacularly. And . . . that's okay! **Nobody's perfect.**

Instead of obsessing over how other people might see you or worrying that they'll laugh at you, just laugh at yourself first. **No one can make fun of you if you're in on the joke.**

YOUR RIGHT TO MAKE MISTAKES

Everybody messes up, feels awkward, or does something embarrassing sometimes. That's part of being a human. You have the right to make a mistake and move on, without it being recorded, posted, or turned into a meme for other people to see.

This means you can ask your friends and your parents not to post photos, videos, or stories about you without your permission. Some moments are meant to stay in the moment.

> If one person starts using their phone, then it's only a matter of time before everyone at the table is on their phone. *—Tyler, 18*

TRY THIS!

Ask your friends to keep smartphones away when you're together so that no one has to worry about being recorded or photographed. (If this makes you feel awkward, you could ask your parents to require people to leave their phones in a basket when they come over, so that the rule doesn't seem like it's coming from you.) Ask for your friends' permission before you take a photo or video of them or post anything online—and ask them to do the same.

WHAT TO DO ABOUT PHOTOGRAPHS

Many rebels enjoy taking photographs with their friends (provided that everyone's okay with it). But they try not to *interrupt* the fun by turning hangouts into photo shoots, and once they've taken the photo, they put the camera away.

When rebels want to share photos with their friends, they do it privately through a text or email, not through social media, where it will be available, sometimes forever, for anyone to see. Some rebels get photos printed and make photo albums and scrapbooks. (Some even use film cameras!)

TRY THIS!

Ask a parent or older relative to show you a scrapbook, photo album, or yearbook from when they were a kid or teenager. Do you notice any differences between their poses and the way people pose for photographs today?

FIND (OR CREATE) A "THIRD PLACE"

A **third place** is somewhere that's not school or home that you and your friends can turn into "your spot": a place where you regularly go to hang out. If you're old enough, find a public spot near you and make it your hangout—for example, a park, bowling alley, pizza place, cafe, mall, or community center.

If your parents think you're too young to be out on your own, ask if you could hang out with your friends at the school playground before or after school. In fact, many schools are starting "play clubs," where kids can sign up to have their after-school activity be having free time on the playground, only lightly supervised and with no structured activities. (If this sounds like fun to you, then ask your teacher or school principal to find out more about play clubs at LetGrow.org.)

You could also ask your parents to make your home or yard into a more fun place for you and your friends to hang out—for example, by putting up a slack line or basketball net, or stocking up on supplies, games, and snacks. Or, if you have the space, you could even build a clubhouse or fort in your (or a friend's) backyard!

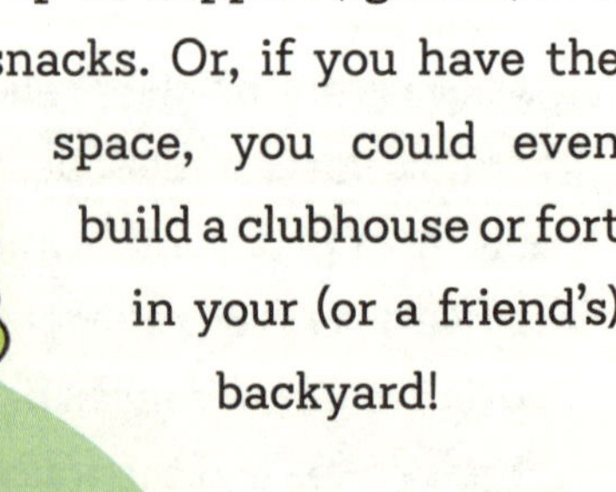

IF SOMETHING IS FUN, DO IT AGAIN

If you try something and like it, do it again. It'll probably be easier to organize the second time around. For example, maybe you can make a tradition out of meeting up on Friday afternoons after school at a particular park, or inviting the same group of friends over on Saturday evenings for a game night or movie.

LESS PHONE = MORE FUN
MORE FUN = LESS PHONE

The more fun I'm having, the less I want to be on my phone. —*Tyler, 18*

Next September
WELCOME BACK STUDENTS!
Yeah, we'll meet after school on Tuesdays!
I've got some hikes planned, and we're also planning an overnight camping trip.
BUG CLUB
ADVENTURE CLUB!

Hi—

!

Hey, Callie.
I missed you this summer.

Um...I was wondering...
Can I join the club too?

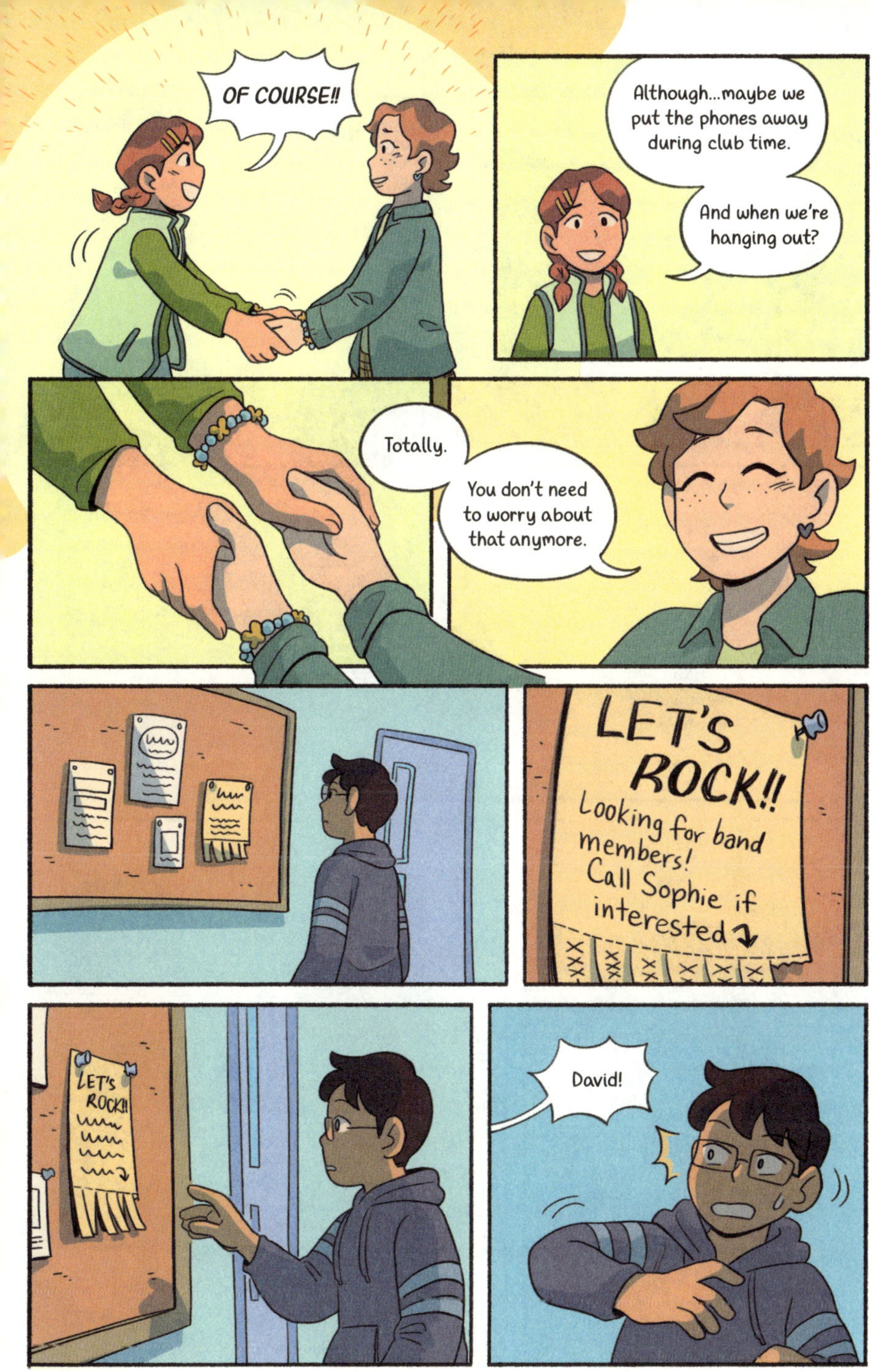

OF COURSE!!

Although...maybe we put the phones away during club time.

And when we're hanging out?

Totally.

You don't need to worry about that anymore.

LET'S ROCK!! Looking for band members! Call Sophie if interested

Are you interested in joining the band??

I–um...

Yeah... I am.

At least, I want to try.

Wait, are there piano players in bands?

Haha, there will be in this one!

Looks like you finally watched the right videos!

Ha. More like I actually started skating...

So, uh...
Can you teach me some tricks sometime?

hmm...

No problem. But I don't really want it recorded or posted online.
Have you seen me skate? I don't want that online either!

Wanna head over now?
Let's go!

click!

haha!

Oh! Isn't that a, um...black-hatted chickpea?
Haha! A black-capped *chickadee*. You were close.

Emma, I'm glad we're hanging out again.

Me too.

Dear Callie,

CONCLUSION
YOUR FUTURE IS IN YOUR HANDS
CONCLUSION

> Being young is the best time of your life. Don't waste it on your phone.
> —*Kendall, 22*

Congratulations: **You now know more about how to take charge of technology and create an amazing life for yourself than most kids—*and* adults.**

You know how much more fun being a kid and teenager was before everyone started spending so much time on screens—and you know how much fun being a kid and teenager could be if people *stopped*.

You know what happened to the people in the generation above yours who got trapped by tech, and you know how to avoid their mistakes.

You know the tech companies' secrets, and that they ultimately need you more than you need them.

You know how to use technology as a tool, and to prevent technology from using *you*.

You know that the best parts of life don't happen on screens.

And you know what awaits you if you choose to join the rebels: ***real* friendship, *real* freedom, and *real* fun.**

So get out there. Try new stuff. Have adventures. Make mistakes.

If you become a rebel, your life won't always be easy. It certainly won't be perfect. But it'll be yours.

And it will be amazing.

SPREAD THE REBELLION

Every time someone decides to become a rebel, the wizards' powers grow weaker. So if you feel inspired (or outraged) by what you've learned in these pages, tell people!

- **TALK TO YOUR FRIENDS AND SIBLINGS**
  If something in this book shocked you, inspired you, or made you mad, share it with a friend or sibling. Tell them the tech companies' secrets and brain-hacking tricks. Explain why the companies' promises are lies. Invite them to join you in having more *real* fun, and not letting smartphones, social media, and video games take over your lives.

- **TALK TO YOUR PARENTS AND GUARDIANS**
  Help the adults in your life understand that if they don't want you and your friends to spend your teen years glued to smartphones, then they need to help you and your friends protect yourselves from addictive technologies and give you more freedom to have fun with your friends in real life.

> I wish I had fought a little harder to keep my other friends off of social media.
> —*Kaylee, 21*

- **TALK TO TEACHERS AND SCHOOL LEADERS**
  Ask your principal (or members of your school's board) to reduce how much technology is used in school, to make the *entire* school day phone-free (including lunch, recess, and between classes), and to start a play club (see page 216). Ask your teachers and coaches not to use social media to communicate any school-related information. And see if you can get your teachers to assign the Let Grow Experience (see page 201).

- **TALK TO COMMUNITY LEADERS AND LEGISLATORS**
  Ask local leaders and elected officials to support laws and rules that protect young people from addictive tech and harmful online content. You can write letters, make phone calls, or even see if there are any in-person meetings that you can attend. Explain how important it is for kids and teens to have phone-free school days and access to safe, fun spaces in the real world where they can grow, play, and learn, without constant digital distractions.

NOTES and SOURCES

You can find the source or link for every claim about research or science, plus parent and teacher guides and more tips on how to handle tech, at: **AmazingGeneration.com.**

LEARN MORE

AnxiousGeneration.com: This is the central website for the movement to roll back the phone-based childhood and restore childhood in the real world.

JonathanHaidt.com: This is Jon's website, where you can learn about his research on the effects of social media on society and on children.

CatherinePrice.com: This is Catherine's website, where you can sign up for her newsletter and learn about her books for adults and older teens, such as *How to Break Up with Your Phone*, and *The Power of Fun*.

AfterBabel.com: This is Jon's Substack, which is basically a blog where he and his team publish research and commentary related to the topics discussed in this book.

CatherinePrice.Substack.com: this is Catherine's "How to Feel Alive" Substack, where she writes about fun, phones, community, and how to have better screen/life balance.

LetGrow.org: This is an organization founded by Jon and by Lenore Skenazy. Here you'll find more information on how to do the Let Grow Experience, and how to set up a play club at your school.

ACKNOWLEDGMENTS

Our first thank-you goes to Cynthia Yuan Cheng, whose vibrant illustrations brought our ideas to life. We thank our wise editor at Penguin Random House, Lauri Hornik, art director Maya Tatsukawa for her beautiful layout, and the amazing team that created the additional design elements of the book: Omou Barry, Xanthe Bouma, and Mary Kate McDevitt. We also thank our agents, Max Brockman and Jay Mandel, and the publicity and marketing team at PRH for sharing this book with the world.

We're grateful to Alexa Arnold, Zach Rausch, and Lenore Skenazy for their thoughtful editing and behind-the-scenes support from beginning to end, as well as to the entire Anxious Generation team for their ideas, feedback, and assistance: Dave Cicirelli, Leeah Derenoncourt, Deb Eschmeyer, Freya India, Ravi Iyer, Katherine Martinko, Matt McInerney, Laura Miller, Casey Mock, Maddy Morris, Elle O'Brien, Maria Petrova, Joanna Rosholm, and Peyton Sterns. Thank you as well to the members of the Tech and Society Lab at NYU Stern who gave us comments and helped with fact checking: Anum Aslam, Nik Greb, Jakey Lebwohl, Jason Lu, Bennett Sippel, and David Stein.

A huge thank-you to all the rebels who shared their personal stories with us: Your quotes, profiles, and experiences are the bedrocks of this book. Thank you as well to the teenagers and young adults who reviewed the manuscript and made it better, including Samara Gorton, Francesca Haidt, Seán Killingsworth, Sophia Lerma, Gabriela Nguyen, Nick Pennington, Tyler Smallwood, Ben Spaloss, and Sophie Stillger, as well as to the parents and kids who provided feedback along the way, including Jenny Connolly, Louise Hartog, Michelle Walker, Alba, Bella, Bennett, Charlotte, Declan, Emlyn, Felix, James, Jane, Jiyoo, Katrina, Lilly, Max, Noah, Parker, Ryder, Sophie, and Theodor. Thanks as well to Grant Griglak, Lisa Kelly, and Alison Wallach for organizing the official PRH focus group, and to all the kids and teens who participated.

A special thank-you to the pediatricians, psychologists, psychiatrists, teachers, and other experts who reviewed the manuscript and helped us make it accurate, effective, and scientifically grounded: Larry Amsel, Bobby Asher, Arturo Bejar, Josh Berezin, Audra Bolhuis, Mariana Brussoni, Sophia Choukas-Bradley, Anna Donnelly, Scott Herman, Beeban Kidron, Mary Edith Leichliter, Anna Lembke, Laura Marquez-Garrett, Chris McKenna, Matthew Murray, Mary Lou O'Grady, Richard Reeves, Nima Rouhanifard, Callie Sopiwnik, and Elizabeth Zack.

We also are grateful to our additional readers who took time out of their schedules to read and comment on the manuscript: Haley Chelemedos, Grace Coll, Michael Dinsmore, Alyssa Fuentes, Jade Garnett, Nicole Kitten, Mckenzie Love, Noah Miller, Kelley Petralia, and Chris Saitta.

Jon adds: I thank Jayne, Max, and Francesca for their love, patience, and ideas as we all tried to figure out how to live with these technologies. I am so grateful to Catherine for her brilliance in figuring out how to convert *The Anxious Generation* into a book that kids would enjoy. It has been great fun to work with you, and I mean "fun" as in real fun.

Catherine adds: In addition to everyone mentioned above, thank you, as always, to my family for their love and support, to Vanessa Gregory for her friendship and editing brilliance, and to P and C: Words can't express my love and gratitude for you both. Most of all, thank you to Jon, not just for your collaborative spirit, your generosity, and for trusting me with this project, but for your wholehearted devotion to rolling back the phone-based childhood and replacing it with one full of real friendship, freedom, and fun. I could not be more grateful.

INDEX